Adapting To What Life Brings

Tom Morris

Thomas Carks∠Brook

Adapting To What Life Brings

Autobiography of B. Tom Morring

Tom Morring
28967 Paseo Picasso
Mission Viejo, Ca. 92692

To order additional copies of this book, contact:
Xlibris Corporation
1-888-795-4274
www.Xlibris.com
Orders@Xlibris.com
89084

Contents

ACKNOWLEDGEMENT

I wish to thank Phyllis Morring, my wife of thirty four years for her love and understanding; Brandt Morring & Melissa Morring, my youngest son and Daughter-in-law; for their love and encouragement in writing this autobiography of my life for all family members' information. Their insistence and curiosity of my life has been my driving force to undertake this almost impossible task.

I also want to express my greatest appreciation and love to my family, past and present; my deceased wife and first love of twenty one years, Lourdes Diangson Morring, our children, Oweni Lourdes Morring, Thomas Norberto Morring, Thom A. Falcon; my present wife, Phyllis Ann Morring, and love of thirty four years and our son, Brandt Richard Morring for the many years they had to tolerate me, work with me, and my obstinacies.

Thanks to my mother, Oene Williams Morring, and my father, Ben T. Morring, for their work ethic, perseverance, character, and drive to make me the best I could be. To my deceased brother, Clyde B. Morring and his family for their help, friendship, and love during all of my life and especially during some of my worst times in life after severe injuries in automobile accidents.

Many thanks to the many people that have been partners, associates, and friends; especially Mike Griffin who has been an energetic, faithful, trusted associate for over twenty four years in my real estate business.

REMEMBER

Your life is only a dash in time from beginning to end,

Your final race in time may be just around the bend.

Remember that only those that love you know what your dash is worth.

It does not matter what possessions you have in life or what they are worth.

What matters is how you live, love, and treat your fellow humans and animals on earth.

Think how life would be; if we slowed down to consider what really matters each day.

Appreciate each other more and keep our anger for another time on our way.

Remember, your dash could end at any time and any place.

Would your friends be pleased with how you spent your dash, in this race?

INTRODUCTION

This book is a summary of the joys and hardships of a Southern Rebel country boy's life from beginning towards the end, sometime in the future. It is an example of living your life, adapting to what happens daily in your life, and the benefits of adapting to events and circumstances that are presented to you. As one songwriter say's: "You have to play the cards that are dealt you".

I have been dealt some very bad hands and had to adapt another opportunity to correct the way. I have also been dealt some very good hands and tried to take advantage of the opportunities that were given. You will understand this in the book as you see me doing so many different things in my life. This is beneficial in many ways since you are forced to become adapted to so many ways of life. All it takes is common sense and much patience.

My life has been so joyful with wonderful life partners and children to keep me continuously working and sharing both good and bad times together. This sharing and enjoying the good and bad times together is what makes life so special and enjoyable to us all. We must, as all of human nature should, enjoy our camaraderie together, in both work and play. Remember each moment together as if it were our last, because you never know, it just might be.

Your "Dash in Time" from beginning to end, is all we have in life. It may be short or it may be long. This is what we never know; therefore we need to make every second count. Think what your loved ones and friends will think of you at the end of your Dash.

My parents taught me in my early years to be truthful, honest, fight for what you believe in, and have a strong work ethic. I have found these to be successful teachings and have tried to teach this to all of my children and hope it carries further to my grand children. I have had many controversies in life because I have always tried to stick to these principles. I have found that the love for money supersedes these philosophies in lots of humans; therefore you have to be on your constant guard.

THE EARLY YEARS

Benjamin Thomas Morring, Jr. was born on a farm near Maysville, Alabama, a community ten miles East of Huntsville, Alabama, on May 13, 1931 of Maye Oene Williams and Benjamin T. Morring, Sr. He had a brother, Clyde and a sister, Alta by his father's deceased first wife. He was delivered by a Dr. Howard, the only practicing physician in the immediate community. Dr. Howard's communication and transportation vehicle was a horse and buggy on gravel or dirt roads. His services were usually paid for in farm products, such as chickens, eggs, fruit, etc. Dr. Howard sold the 56 acre farm adjoining Flint River, as raw land, to my dad in 1927 for $65 payable at $5 quarterly until paid. Flint River in Alabama covers approximately 568 Square miles and is a tributary to the Tennessee River. The area covers predominately agriculture.

Dr. Howard also owned farmland and his farms were operated by his unmarried sister in law, Martha. They also raised prime cattle and always had a champion bull for service to the public for a fee of twenty five to fifty cents. On one well reported time a local farmer brought his cow to be serviced by the doctor's bull. Martha stood by while the cow was being serviced. The farmer remarked that he would like to do that and Martha told him to go ahead, it was his cow. There was always some comedy in country life. The community of Maysville consisted of two grocery stores and gas stations, a cotton gin, and numerous homes. It was a typical rural farm community.

Thomas or Tom, as I am commonly known, has first memory of life at approximately two years old. This memory was me seeing our dog, Spot, being brought out from under our house as a baby puppy with his mother Lit, an ornery hound. Spot grew up a friendly, but belligerent, dog that had a pastime of running every other dog out of the area of his momentary acquired territory. My father, Ben, operated the Maysville cotton gin as ginner for five dollars per week. Spot would sometimes, all alone, go the half mile to Ben at the cotton gin. He would first walk around the village and run any other dogs in the village home, possibly whipping them first, and then go lay by the cotton gin near dad and go to sleep. He always had to clear his territory. Sometimes a stray dog would come near our home and Spot would whip them and run them across Flint River, which adjoined our farm on the West. After the fight and chase was over he would go hunting for rabbits in the river bottom after which he would come back home.

My mother's parents moved from Tennessee to live with us in late 1937. My grandmother, Mary Elizabeth Burch Williams, was getting old and was having heart trouble and my grandfather, Henry Harrison Williams could no longer take care of their farm. My mother and father agreed to take care of them and their other daughters would contribute a total of sixty five dollars per month for their care. Their farm was rented out to another farmer and their old home would be kept vacant for the single daughters to have a place to stay when they were not teaching school. It was fun having my grandparents around. My grandmother passed away in March 1938.

FATHER AND SON 1935

My grandfather was a lot of fun to be around and he taught me how to play Chinese checkers, regular checkers, and card games including poker. It was lots of fun playing poker with my dad, my grandpa, and my mother on weekends and at night. Grandpa also taught me how to shoot a .22 caliber rifle. He liked to shoot the sparrows that were always eating the chicken feed and my dad appreciated that since the feed was very expensive. My grandfather did not have any teeth and it was a treat watching him eat corn on the cob. He had no problems with that. I well remember grandmother's sister, Aunt Dollie Burch, and her sausage. When she came for grandmother's funeral she brought some of her and Uncle Willie's sausage for the family. My mother made me sandwiches for school with biscuits and sausage. They were so hot I could not eat them. Other students gave me part of their lunch that day.

Aunt Dollie and her brother, Uncle Willie, lived together on his farm in Tennessee and neither of them was ever married. In 1942 grandfather moved back to Tennessee to his home, since my mother started teaching again, and Aunt LeVert took care of him until his death in 1944. He and grandmother were buried in Pulaski, Tennessee.

Sometimes we would get sick with colds or whatever. The treatment, in those days, was a dose of quinine, or a cough syrup made of chocolate syrup and quinine, or a small dose of bourbon and kerosene, therefore you seldom got sick. If you were capable of taking those medicines, you were certainly sick.

We would go to the local Baptist church approximately twice a year and usually participated in the fourth of July barbecue or some other community activity. This was usually fun, but I got very sick one time after a church barbecue or dinner, outside at a cousins house, in the summertime. I have never seen so many flies in one place in my life. The house was about two hundred feet from the barn on the farm. I never went back there again.

I got my first pair of bib overalls, from my brother, on my sixth birthday. When I asked him what he had gotten me, he said a pair of kitten britches. I kept pestering him until he jumped our front yard fence and went to visit his girlfriend, approximately ten miles away. He was always teasing me about something and that make him the best brother anyone could have.

Farm life was great but very demanding. I began milking cows, after my father taught me how, at the early age of six. The fun part of the milking was squirting fresh milk into the mouth of kittens that always came around when milking was done. There were always cats in the barn to catch mice and rats that frequented the corn cribs. I began plowing cotton also at the age of six with my father's favorite small mule, Mandy, who knew more about plowing than most farm hands. She walked slow and when she got to the end of the row she would turn around very slowly, without instruction, ready to start down the next row. She would stop and wait until I was ready and continue down another row. Sometimes I would go to the river bottoms with my father to plow corn. While my father plowed with a cultivator and a couple of mules, I would help when needed and try to fish in the slews with a cane and line and a straight pin for a hook, using earthworms. This was recreation while working. Everyone always took Sundays off to study and play. A normal day's work, during school days, was to milk the cows, slop the hogs, turn the cows to the pasture and make sure there was plenty of water at the house for the day's housework. The water was carried from our well, approximately one hundred yards to the house, in buckets, and stored in two Double Cola thirty gallon barrels for the days use in cooking, baths, or canning fruit from the orchard and garden. In the afternoon after school I would bring more water, cut more kindling and wood for the wood stove, bring in the cows by horseback, milk, feed the stock including the hogs, and study after dark, sometimes until after midnight. They were my after school jobs until I was approximately twelve years old. At that time, even though World War II was on, my father was able to get a new Oliver tractor. I then would take shifts with my father at night plowing the farm. In the springtime Dad would plow approximately sixteen hours a day and I would plow six to eight hours at night, get a couple more hours of sleep and go to school.

During the spring, before plowing began, my father would park a wagon by the horse stalls in the barn and tell me to dig out the manure, with a pick and shovel, and fill the wagon. He then would take it into the garden and unload it and bring the wagon back for me to fill again. This cleaned out the stalls for the livestock as well as fertilizing the garden. This is one job that was very hard and I hated it very much.

During the canning and fruit season there was always fruit and vegetables to pick. Until I was about nine years old, I was not allowed to peel fruit or cut vegetables for fear of cutting myself. When the fruit and produce was picked, in supply enough that mother and the colored ladies had enough to do, I was allowed to play with the helps children for a while. This was about the only time I had any children to play with while I was growing up except when I was at school. It was a hard, but good life for all. I never thought about being bored, as children do today, because I would be told to bring water, cut wood, or bring in wood for heating and cooking, go feed the hogs or work in the garden or someplace.

Flour came in twenty five pound sacks. A bag of flour cost twenty five cents. Normal daily wage for farm work was fifty cents per day. A day's work was from sun up to sun down. I remember my mother saving flour sacks and making dresses out of them. Fertilizer sacks were saved and sheets for the bed were made from them and sometimes men's working shirts.

When I was about ten years old my dad would go for a walk with me on Sundays and teach me how to track rabbits, squirrels, possums, cattle, horses, and birds in the fields and woods. This was an interesting lesson and of great value to me as I grew up and started hunting. It was also used later in life to track humans on occasion as needed. He also taught me how to trap predatory animals with steel traps. We used these to keep animals from stealing our chickens, turkeys, guineas, and sometimes in hunting for food.

Early in life I wanted to fix everything I saw, mechanically. One time my cousin gave me a Big Ben watch for my birthday. These were usually called dollar watches because that was the price. I immediately had to take it apart and see how it was made and try to fix it. Of course it was impossible for me to fix after I took it all apart. Other times, as I got some older, it became my job to fix the heater in the automobile, a 1939 Dodge coupe. The heater had always given trouble and after my disassembly many times, I finally got it fixed. This began my life as a mechanic, equipment operator, machinist, farmer, business manager, electrician, store operator, public works superintendant, real estate broker, property manager, court receiver, and generally a jack of all trades.

Of course, in those days, women cooked on wood fired stoves. Temperatures were never stable and my mother burned lots of bread, cakes, cookies, and food in general. I usually had the opportunity to eat all of the burned food that I wanted and was required to eat all food that was fixed at mealtime. If you did not like a certain food you had to learn to like it.

Grandpa would make homemade wine from our grape vineyard. I soon found where he kept it stored and I helped him drink it, unbeknownst to him or anyone else. I am sure he missed some of the wine, but he never told anyone. What a nice man.

My dad would grow produce in the garden and he would take the extra produce, fruit, and chickens to the farmers market in Huntsville in the spring or fall of the year. He would take the merchandise the ten miles to Huntsville by horse and wagon. He would leave home about four AM and go the ten plus miles to the market and get set up for opening at seven AM. Sometimes I would go with him and help. This was a chore that I really enjoyed.

I was lucky, and the Kiwanis club gave me a female pig with the stipulation that I would give back two female pigs when they were born.

Luck again because the sow gave birth to twenty one pigs the first litter. She could only nurse sixteen babies at one time, therefore five of them had to be bottle fed. One later died. I was offered five hundred dollars for the sow by another local doctor, but refused the offer. The sow's next litter was nineteen little pigs, of which three had to be bottle fed. I later bought two prize Black Angus bulls from my great uncle in Tennessee and made one a steer and a show animal for the County Fair and sold him there. My high school agriculture teacher taught me how to castrate male cows and pigs. I also tried bull riding of this steer and it did not work so well. I was thrown into a woodpile and hurt pretty bad. I kept the bull for breeding purposes and Tarbaby II served me well.

Our farm consisted of a one acre house site with a hand dug water well, with a three bedroom, kitchen, dining room, an outhouse, five acre horse and cow lot with barn, one and a half acre garden, six acre fruit orchard and pig area, three acre potato patch, ten acre pine woods and pasture, twenty nine and a half acre cotton, corn, and hay land. My father rented additional farm land in the community for growing cotton and corn. In 1943 my parents purchased an additional fifty acres of river bottom land for growing corn and hay.

One of my most despised farm jobs was hauling and storing hay for the ten to twenty five cattle and horses to eat in the wintertime. My brother Clyde, who was 18 years older and the son of my father and his deceased first wife, loved to try to cover me up with hay, on the wagon. He and one farm hand would put the shocks of hay on the wagon together and I would have to place them around the wagon to equalize the load. When the day was over everyone would be covered with itchy hay chaff and would go to the river and go swimming to clean up. One time I was in the loft, of the barn, throwing the hay back and they covered me up. I had bad asthma when I was growing up and my dad came to see what the problem was. I was not throwing the hay back, and he found me passed out from the chaff and the heat in the loft of the barn. That was the last time that I had to work in the loft. In the summer time and early fall it was my job to help out wherever in the fields. I did not chop any cotton but I picked cotton all day at picking time. I got one cent per pound for picking. At first I made fifteen cents a day but finally got up to a dollar as I got older. I graduated from the cotton picking when my father got the tractor. More intelligent work thereafter, thank goodness. I also bought me a used Schwinn bicycle for twelve dollars. This made my getting around much easier and I rode six miles each way to summer school that year.

After my father bought the river bottom land we would run cattle there in the fall and winter to eat any corn or other grain that might have been left on the ground. One time, early in the spring, it started raining hard and continued all night. My father was unable at that time to do much work because he had cancer. He woke me up and told me to get the horse and find the cattle, and get them out of the river bottom, because it was going to flood. I tried to give an argument because it was about three in the morning and raining. He made his point, physically, and I got my horse and went after the cattle. After I found them the river was already rising and at some points the horse and cattle had to swim to get out of the river bottom. That was the last time I ever challenged my father on anything.

When my brother was still at home he and my father and a couple of farm hands would take his boat and go frog gigging at night. They would usually come back with a sack full of large bull frogs and we would have frog's legs for a day of two. In those day, we were always looking for game for food.

One year, during the winter months when farm work was slow, I decided to build a row boat for playing in the Flint River and for fishing as my brother had done when he was younger. I built a sixteen foot, flat bottom, row boat and kept it tied up by the river bridge, in our horse pasture, near our house. I used it mostly just paddling around to get away from the house and do some trot line fishing in the river. One day I went to get my boat and it was gone. From the river bridge I saw it being paddled up the river by a neighbor boy. I asked for him to bring it back but he told me where to go. I went home and got the shotgun and shot at him from the bridge. He jumped out of the boat and I caught it as it floated back down the river. His parents called the Sheriff and told them I tried to kill him. The Sheriff came to my dad and I explained what had occurred. I was given a good lecture and told to not do that again.

I met the neighbor friend in a bar, several years later, when I got out of the Army, and he tried to bring up the subject again. I told him to lets just go outside and finish the argument. He just stood and looked at me for a while and said "let's just have a beer". Over the years he had grown to be a much bigger man than I, so I do not know what he thought. A couple of weeks later he had his stomach cut open by a small man and almost died.

My first driving lesson was driving our new Oliver tractor at age of twelve. I then began hauling fuel for the tractor to the fields with our car for my father. I started driving the auto on the gravel roads at fourteen with my mother, going back and forth to school, and took my drivers test on my sixteenth birthday and got my drivers license.

Our two bed room, one outhouse home was remodeled into a two story, 5 bedroom, 2 bath home and we got electricity in 1945. When the home was remodeled we installed electrical wiring even though electricity was not available at that time. I wired the house myself with diagrams and instructions from a Montgomery Ward Catalogue. When the power line was finally built they connected to my wiring, without any change, and it stayed that way until I left for military service in 1950. I also traded my bicycle in for a Whizzer motor bicycle at this time and it made it still easier to get around if I had to go somewhere.

I remember one time we went to Tennessee to visit my grandparents and when we got home one of our farm hands was standing guard outside our home with a shotgun. He said we never left home overnight and he was guarding the property because he found the front door unlocked. No one locked their homes in those days but he was protecting it because we were away. My dads' farm hands were very dedicated to him and were always looking out for his interest. He would show his appreciation for their dedication by giving them fruit, vegetables, meat when hogs were butchered, and shares of the crops and they would in turn bring us rabbits, squirrels, possum, etc.

I went to Central Elementary School, which was one mile from my home, through the fourth grade. My father was on the school board there when he met my mother to be. She was teaching at the school. Even though this school was close to home, it was across the Flint River from home, and in the winter floods the school bus would have to go approximately six miles around because the road would be flooded. When I was in the first grade, my teacher Miss Williams (no relation) thought I was very smart and I therefore got all A's for grades. Second grade teacher was Mrs. Kennedy, and I did well there also. Third and fourth grade teacher was Mrs. Mellette, a cousin by marriage, of my dads'. I did very well in school under her tutelage also. I also had a part in a school play and I enjoyed it very much. The next year my mother started teaching school again and I transferred to Riverton High School some six miles away from home. I remember gasoline prices at that time were fifteen cents per gallon. My mother would put one dollar of gas in the car on Monday morning to last all week. Because of World War II gasoline was rationed. Farmers and teachers got extra coupons to buy gasoline, so we always had enough for our needs.

I do not remember who my fifth grade teacher was but grades were good, however, because my mother was a teacher at that school, I was in constant trouble. My classmates learned that I would always get a whipping if they would report that I was smoking. My mother was always told immediately and she would insist that I go before the principle of the school. At first he would whip me and later, when he found out what was going on, he only made me sit in his office for a period. My mother would do the whipping when I got home. The school had an outside restroom, some one hundred yards from the classrooms; therefore it was known to be an unsupervised place for lots of misbehavior by students.

My sixth grade was with my mother as teacher. Not one of my best years. I was not allowed good grades that year, whatever I earned, because mother thought she was prejudicial if I got better grades than other students. I quit trying to make good grades therefore. During this year I started taking public speaking classes to get out of her room as much as possible. It also helped polish my voice from the early ages of hog calling. Toward the end of the year I won several county public speaking contests and I loved it. I was hooked. The next year I went to the state public speaking finals.

I continued at that school through the ninth grade when my mother transferred to another school and then I rode the school bus for the first time in five years. I also traded my Whizzer bicycle in and bought a near new Indian Motorcycle. I then went to Madison County High School at Gurley, Alabama. This school was approximately eight miles from home and was in the area we lived. I did well through the tenth grade and especially remember Mr. Elliott, my algebra and geometry teacher. He was an exceptional math teacher and I made all A's in his classes. He gave me the basis for math for the rest of my life. My most despised classes in school were history. I have never thought we should dwell on yesterday, but look for tomorrow. I decided at the end of that year that I wanted to graduate the next year. I had enough credits at the end of my eleventh year. I enjoyed both the tenth and eleventh grades because I went out for football and also got a job part of my eleventh year driving the school bus, since I lived near the end of the route and had gotten my drivers license on my sixteenth birthday. I also got a main part in the senior play with Joan, a cute and feisty girl. It was a great year except for an English teacher that didn't care for me and hated my mother for some reason. She flunked me in English so I could not graduate. I finished school that summer by taking English in summer school in Huntsville, and made all A's in the six week course, therefore graduating. The best part of the year was being able to take, Iris, the prettiest girl in the class to the senior prom night and dancing with her. All of the sports jocks had tried to date her and when I asked her she accepted. It was a great night and when I took her home we danced some more in her living room. Her parents were big farmers with a cotton gin and were well thought of in their community. After high school she went to college and I was told that she married a farmer from South Alabama.

I had already planned my college program. I would go to Draughons Business School in Nashville, Tennessee. When I finished there I could get a job and work myself through Law School. My parents could subsidize my business school at twenty five dollars a month, therefore I got a job as soon as I enrolled. The school found me a place to stay for twenty five dollars a month, room and two meals daily, at a boarding house across the street from Vanderbuilt University. I found a job at Candyland, an ice cream, cake, sandwich, and candy shop, near Draughons in the center of town. I got one meal daily there. I went to school eight hours daily and worked six hours at Candylands. Sometimes Candyland would be short of help behind the soda fountain or for cleaning up and I would work until they closed at midnight. In this case I had to walk home seventeen blocks because the buses quit running at midnight.

During one period of time I got laid off at Candyland because of lack of seniority and was looking for a job. I was at a Standard Oil service station and the owner was working alone and was very busy. I started helping pump gas and after about an hour the owner told me he could not afford to pay for another attendant. I told him I did not expect pay and was just helping because it looked like he needed help. He later hired me to work a couple of hours on weekends and then asked if I would like to drive a race car. He had a car they used for jalopy races at Cumberland Speedway. He offered twenty five dollars if I would drive one weekend. I accepted and did the race and was rammed by another car and took the car through the fence of railroad crossties in the process. He paid me anyway and I worked some more weekends pumping gas for him until I got back to regular work. It was my first experience at fast driving.

In approximately October of that year I looked up at my work, at Candyland, and my father was entering the door. He looked terrible. He said I had to come back home because his cancer had gotten worse and he needed me at home. That was the end of my school and I went home with him and he died two months later.

I met Nira Caskey, a beautiful and nice girl, while working at Candyland and we dated for several months by going to the park near her home and visiting or going to the movies. We liked to just go to the park and sit by the lake and talk for hours. Her mother and father were separated and her father tried to get me to quit school and go to Texas and work with him in the oil fields. Of course I declined, because I wanted to finish school. Her mother seemed to like me and encouraged me to visit her daughter. After I went home with my father, Nira wrote me several letters, but I never knew until after my father died. My mother tore them up without me seeing them, because she said I was too young to be seeing girls. When I discovered what had been done I went back to Nashville to see Nira and found she had married someone and had been killed in an apparent suicide auto accident. While in Nashville my mother reported my car stolen and I was stopped by the police and locked up for a couple of days while they investigated. A police detective, a friend of my father, came to get me and took me back home with my car.

I then got a job at the shoe plant in Huntsville for a couple of months until I decided to enlist in the Army Paratroopers. My mother insisted that she buy me a couple of mules and I should begin farming the homestead, since that was all I was good for. I informed her I was eighteen and she could not stop me from going into the service. She tried to get the enlistment personnel to stop the enlistment and was told there was nothing she could do.

The County Fair was being held in Huntsville and one night I decided to go to the fair alone. During my walk around the fairground a young lady came over and grabbed my arm and asked if I wanted company. I of course said sure and we spent the rest of the evening going through the fair together. I took her home later and got a date with her for the next night and we went to the movies. She was a drummer for the Huntsville High School Band. A nice personality but cross eyed. That was the last date I had with her and after that I found notes on my car whenever I parked in downtown Huntsville. Her mother was a nurse at the local hospital. After all of the notes, it was time to go.

On the way to report to the recruiting office for duty my mother had a wreck with another automobile at an intersection. It was the other drivers fault but I was about to be late to report to the Army. The Highway Patrol took me to the recruiting office so I would not be late. My mother later got her car fixed and she was back to teaching.

MILITARY LIFE

I sold my car and joined the Army on February 1, 1950. I, along with other enlistees, was sent approximately sixty five miles to Gadsden, Alabama for the night. We were put in a hotel for the night to depart for Fort Knox, Kentucky the next day. Our hotel stay was tragic. I felt things crawling over me during the early night and when I turned on the light there were lice everywhere. I got up, put on my clothes, and spent the rest of the night sitting in the lobby. We shipped out the next day by train to our destination. We all had physicals the next day after arrival in Fort Knox, Kentucky. I noticed some enlistees were turned down because of flat feet. When I went through for my physical, the doctor pulled me out and asked for me to walk across the room. Since I was flatfooted I arched up my feet and walked across the room. The doctor said if I wanted into the army that bad he would let me go.

About four weeks into basic training all personnel were given an IQ test. The testing lasted for two days. Approximately one week later certain personnel were called in and given the results of the test and the opportunity to go to Officers Training School. If you graduated from there you would be given the commission as second lieutenant. I was told that my IQ test showed a 150+ grade, very high for potential officer material, however I declined because I just wanted to be a regular soldier. I had heard a lot of tales about second lieutenants.

Basic training was very hard since I was severely out of shape since school. I weighed one hundred thirty five pounds. I trained hard and after two weeks I was promoted to Lance Sergeant to help the regular Army personnel in training. I suppose my voice carried well because I had learned to call hogs early in life. Since I had joined the Army Paratroopers unassigned, I was really trying hard and wanted to be the best. My desire to join the paratroopers was initiated when I got the opportunity to fly with a young man in a J-3 Piper Cub airplane one time when I was fourteen years old. Flying was my main desire from then on, but on graduation from High School I found you had to be a college graduate to be a military pilot. So the paratroopers were the next best thing. I would get to fly, but I had to jump out of a perfectly good airplane to do it, on a regular schedule.

I continued until I finished basic training. Several on my group wanted to go to the paratroopers but I was the only lucky one, since I had enlisted for Airborne beforehand. I then was transferred to Fort Benning, Georgia for airborne training. I had thought basic training was hell. I found the airborne was worse. You started at 5:00 AM and continued all day, sometimes even into the night. After four weeks of physical training and learning how to fall, we then went to the thirty four foot towers to jump. The procedure in the towers were the orders to stand up, hook up, and when instructor touched you on the back, you jumped. You felt the shock since you fell fifteen feet before your static line caught the cable and took you out to the end of cable. On one occasion a Lieutenant forgot to hook up and jumped. After falling the thirty four feet to the ground, he staggered up, turned around, and stated, "if this gets worse I'm going to quit". I do not remember but I think he made it. After training on low towers we then were pulled up on the two hundred foot towers and released to float to the ground and land like a sack of potatoes. We then went on to jump out of airplanes for our first jump. If you had the heart after that you were thought to be in and made more jumps. My third jump was the scariest of all. You knew what it was like but you were not confident yet that you were not going to be killed.

After graduation from jump school I was assigned as a run instructor for training. This required you to run twenty five miles daily with airborne recruits and sometimes as many as three times daily. After going through all of this training I weighed one hundred ninety four pounds. I got a weekend leave one week and went home to see my brother on his farm near Brownsboro, Alabama. My brother was almost blind since his eighteenth birthday, but his hearing was incredible. He heard me walking on the gravel driveway and knew my walk and came running to meet me. Being a smart ass, I grabbed him and put him on my shoulder. We had a great weekend visit and I went back to camp. A couple of months later, on my twenty seventh jump, I pulled a streamer and my emergency chute collapsed approximately two hundred feet before ground. I hit a tree and stripped the limbs down one side, breaking my collarbone, arm, and injuring my back. After the hospital stay I went back up to jump again and I could not.

The Korean War had then started and I was ordered to Seattle, Washington for shipment to Korea. We flew to Japan via Anchorage, Alaska, Aleutian Islands, on to Haneda Air Base in Tokyo, Japan. We started with two planes of troops and landed in Japan with one. I never knew what happened with the other plane. I was initially sent to Camp Zama for a couple of weeks. We had nothing to do, so we found out how to go out the back fence into town each night and have a few beers. I was then transferred to Camp Drake where I was assigned to Military Police motorcycle escort for convoys to Yokohama on their way to Korea. One night on this duty, without much sleep, I went to sleep on the motorcycle and woke up just as I was going through the wall of a sake shop and out into a rice paddy. That was the end of my convoy duty.

They were training a new force to go to Korea. Mostly ex-marines, ex—paratroopers, and under water demolition troops for advance party invasion. I volunteered and was accepted because of my airborne training. We trained hard for a month before the Inchon invasion. This invasion was a scary part that I prefer to forget. Shortly after the invasion I got hysterical one night, from an incident, and my sergeant from basic training showed up and slapped the hell out of me and I was ok from then on. Nothing much bothered me. During a village cleanout, as I was going up the stairs, a party came out the upstairs door and fired at me. I dived down the stairs, but caught a bullet, from a burp gun, in the back of my neck. I did not think it was bad and ignored it. Some days later it got worse and I started having a fever. I got a drink of water from a rice patty and soon thereafter the medics checked me out and determined I had malaria also, and sent me back to Japan. After a short stay in the hospital, I found out that one of my friends had been killed. While on a three day pass, I got some forged orders sending me back to my old outfit. When I reported back the commanding officer looked at the orders, laughed and said if I was that stupid I was going out on patrol that night. I continued my combat duty for another two months when we were on the East side of the Chosen Reservoir in North Korea. This is the coldest place on earth in November and December. This was the coldest I have ever been in my life. Temperatures were ten to forty degrees below zero at night and many troops had severe frostbite on their hands and feet. I have loved the California desert ever since. I then got shrapnel in my left kneecap and was sent back to Japan again to the hospital. They replaced my kneecap.

TOM MORRING 1951

I was born of Protestant religion but I noticed while in the hospital that the Catholic priest was the only one that came around to see us and he would visit everyone. At that time I decided to become a Catholic and in later years was baptized in the Catholic Church.

When I got out of the hospital I was put on Military Police duty for a while. I got into an argument with the Commanding Officer because he would not let me go back to Korea. In the process I did the unforgivable, and slapped him. He immediately took my Sergeants stripes and I got my transfer. I was sent to Korea again as a Military Policeman. While on MP duty one evening at a checkpoint, I observed an old lady of unusually large bulk coming toward us and I got an uneasy feeling. I yelled for everyone to take cover just as the old lady exploded. She had been loaded with grenades under her clothing, creating her large bulk. A couple of personnel were injured and she was killed, of course, from the explosion. If she had come any further many of us at the checkpoint would probably have been killed.

This time my stay was short, until I was transferred back to Japan. I was assigned back to the Military Police and shortly was assigned to work as an undercover drug agent. During this duty I made a trip to Hong Kong. That was an interesting trip but very short. Someone took a shot at me in the hotel and I left the next day on orders. As I was leaving the hotel the next morning, a shot took the corner out of a building just by my head. It was surely time to go. I caught the next plane back to Japan. Shortly thereafter another agent and I had a confrontation with a drug runner and we turned in a large amount of cash and twenty five pounds of Opium. I also made trips to Brisbane, Australia; Jakarta, Indonesia; Saigon, Vietnam; Manila, Philippines; and Singapore, in Southeast Asia. I was then assigned to Military Police duty at an engineer base in Tokyo.

This was a nice relaxed duty. We were questioned everyday, after we dressed out and before duty, by the Officer of the Day or Provost Marshall. Questions were usually on the government and the constitution. I was exceptionally good with answers, and the one that got the most right answers got the day off. I had a lot of days off and a lot of time to get in trouble. We had to have newly cleaned uniforms every day and I found a laundry a block from our base that was run by a Japanese family. The young lady that was manager was Kimico Igarashi, the youngest daughter. She seemed to like me and therefore I asked her for a date to go to the movies one night that I was off. She accepted with the condition we go to the opera instead. It was the first opera I had ever been to and it was fantastic. We went to many more opera's for the next couple of months or we would just sit by the counter of the laundry and talk. She was about ten years older than I, but fun to visit with. They were a fine and gracious family, always friendly and helpful. Through her I met a lady that owned the Coca Cola franchise on Honshu. She tried to get me to get out of the Army and work for her franchise. I declined because I still had a lot of Army time to do. Kimico finally married a soldier from Colorado. I met her again in Los Angles in 1954 and we visited for about an hour. She was working for a family in Hollywood as housekeeper and her husband had reenlisted in the Army. This was the last I ever saw of her. She was a good friend.

During this period I started taking Judo lessons with another Military Policeman. It was hard training but very satisfying and productive. I had neglected to go to training for a few days and just went into Tokyo and goofed off. One day when I was coming out of the base my Japanese instructor was waiting for me outside the gate. He informed me that I was going to Judo practice as I was supposed to. I told him I would go tomorrow. He got me by the arm, very hard, and said again that we were going to training. Of course I went and when we dressed out and started practice he would throw me to the mat. I would get up and he would throw me to the mat again. This continued for about two hours. He then let me get a cold shower and said he would meet me again the next day, which he did. This old instructor was over eighty years old. He had given President Theodore Roosevelt lessons in the Washington White House when he was young. I kept at the training and eventually got the first degree of the Black Belt prior to leaving Japan.

The Commanding Officer called me in one day. He had gotten a letter from my mother demanding that I write home. I told him that I was not going to write. My mother and I had plenty of words before I joined the Army. His reply was "you little bastard" at which I leaped over the desk at him. He was sitting in a swivel chair in front of a large, low window. We were both catapulted out the window down two floors to the concrete sidewalk. I was not hurt. He was not so lucky and spent approximately seven months in the hospital. I was taken to jail and eventually tried, and convicted for aggravated assault. My sentence was three years in confinement and a Dishonorable Discharge. I was lucky again and had the last word. My defense counsel tried to bring out what the officer had called me that caused my response. The judge would not allow it to be put in the record or consider it. However the court clerk, apparently forget to take it out. When it got to appellate review in Washington, they ordered me back to duty. After nine months and twenty seven days I was returned to duty and after finishing my tour of duty was given a General Discharge under Honorable Conditions.

After the trial I was taken to Big Eight prison in Japan. The stay there was about ninety days. As usual I smarted off to someone and got thirty days in solitary confinement. When I was ready to go back to my regular quarters an officer asked me if I had learned to behave. I replied, yes sir. As they opened the door to let me out, I hit the officer in the face, and I was put back in for another thirty day stay. Some ten days later the Inspector General came by and asked how long I was in for. I replied that I was in for my second thirty consecutive day sentence. That is not allowed therefore I was released to go back to my cell. Shortly thereafter I was given orders to transfer to Camp Cook, Lompoc, California to continue serving my sentence. I found that my old partner in the Military Police CID was aboard ship. Several days out at sea it was discovered he had fallen overboard and was not found. I was immediately given an armed guard, by my cell aboard ship, to make sure I made it back to the United States alive. When I got to Camp Cook and was evaluated I was assigned to finance as a bookkeeper. I had taken a course through UCLA in bookkeeping to refresh what I had learned in college. After five days at work I was again transferred to Harrisburg, Pennsylvania and assigned to hospital duty. When I first arrived there one morning, at breakfast in the mess hall, a black man used the spoon that he had just taken out of his mouth to dip in a peanut butter jar that was for everyone and I asked if he wanted the peanut butter stuck up his ass. He gave some smart remark and I hit him with a coffee mug knocking him cold. I spent another day in solitary confinement. Then I got assigned to the base hospital. There I received much better services and worked for a female nurse, Captain Cheesman, who was nice to work for. She got me permission to eat with the staff in the officers' mess hall. I would go back to my cell at night to retire. This procedure was continued until I was told I was going back to duty. At this point I was transferred to Leavenworth, Kansas to go through training again before going back to duty. During the training period we got weekend passes if we behaved. I went into town each weekend and tried to drink Kansas dry. Approximately ten months without a beer or any outside activity, was too much. Sometimes I would buy a six pack and just go for a walk in the country. I just wanted to be alone.

When we graduated we were asked where we wanted to be stationed. I again answered Japan and thought that was where I was going. We shipped out from San Francisco and I found out where I was going after we left Hawaii. Anywhere was good to me except duty in the United States. We arrived in Manila, Philippines and they took us to Cavite City for assignment. I was again given Military Police duty. We were a small detachment with our own Provost Marshall's office, staff offices, two jail cells, and our sleeping quarters near the officers' compound. There was a nice large mango tree over our offices and it was an excellent source for great fresh fruit and a new food experience for me.

My duty assignment was as a patrol officer in and around Cavite City and Sangley Point, an adjoining naval base. Our patrol duties were usually one Army Military Police and a Navy Shore Patrol because the Army MP's were allowed to wear guns and the Navy SP's were not, therefore we were protecting each other. Sometimes this was a good arrangement. One time my partner and I went into an upstairs bar and a fight had just started. A sailor decided to show the army who was boss and hit me with a chair.

My SP partner immediately grabbed the sailor, hit him with a club while I was getting up, and we both threw him down the stairs. When he got up we had the hand cuffs on him and put him in the SP van. In about two minutes he tore the back door off the van and jumped out right into the face of my forty-five pistol. We radioed for backup and he was taken to Sangley Point lockup. Another time at a local bar a soldier accosted me with a beer bottle and my SP associate took it away from him. He tried to then attack me with a knife and cut my right arm slightly. I immediately tried to beat him to death with my custom made Mahogany night stick. My commanding officer got a report of this and gave me a good lecture in self control. I thought I was just protecting myself. Another incident involved a marine from Sangley Point. We observed him pick up this girl, commonly known as a bennie boy because it was not a girl but a man, dressed as a girl. They got into a taxi, or jeepney as they were commonly known because they were World War II jeeps that had been restored for civilian use as taxis. We stopped the jeepney and asked the marine what he was doing. He stated he had found this girl and they were going on a date. I asked him, "do all of your girl friends wear combat boots"? He looked down at her feet for the first time. His face got very red and he said shit and got out of the jeepney. We took him back into town and let him go. He thanked us and walked away.

Sometimes we would get duty on the base front gate which had two gates. There was one gate for walk in personnel, and one for traffic. This one time I was the ranking MP so I got the personnel gate assignment. A certain amount of ladies were allowed to come in to meet boy friends for dancing at the enlisted men's club. They had to sign in, and state who they were going to see. This one girl came to the gate and asked for permission to go in to see her guy. The MP on the traffic gate came over to me and told me not to let her in. I told him to get back on his post and tend to his own business. He pulled his gun on me and repeated not to let her in. I told him OK to go back to his post. As he put his gun up I shot him in the foot. He yelped and hobbled back to his post. I called the MP office and told them what had happened. They relieved him from duty and took him to the hospital in Sangley Point. I finished my shift and then had to make a report. This soldier never challenged me again nor did anyone else. I did not get into trouble for the act.

Another time, when I was working as desk sergeant, we got a call that a soldier was causing trouble at the EM Club. I went on the call and found a soldier, an American Indian by descent and a very muscular and big guy, drunk and picking a fight. I sure did not want to get into a beef with him so I talked him into leaving with me in the jeep to go home. When we got to the MP office he did not want to get out of the jeep because that was not where he lived. I talked him into going into the MP office and I locked him up for the night. Chief, as he was called, thanked me the next day and we let him out without charges.

One day the operations sergeant asked if anyone would volunteer to make a trip to Subic Bay and bring back an unusual truck load of materials for the engineers to use in the bay. He said anyone that would volunteer would get a three day pass after they got back. Several asked what the load was and what they were driving. He said the engineers needed explosive material to clear the wreckage in the bay and the load was nitro and a semi. I was the only one that volunteered. When we got there the load was ready. A fifty gallon drum, on a rope hammock on the bed of a semi Mack truck. I was told that the MP escort would be between five and ten miles ahead of me and another five miles behind me. I should get it up to sixty miles an hour and keep it there. They would clear the way, which they did nicely. I was told afterwards that if something went wrong, and it exploded, there would be nothing left but a hole in the ground. I delivered the merchandise and took my three day pass and stayed drunk.

Our senior MP staff was an excellent but strange mix of personnel. The Provost Marshall was a Captain that had never seen combat duty, but had been an attorney in civilian life. He was an excellent commander and very reasonable. Our Provost Sergeant was a Reserve Colonel with a first sergeant's permanent rating, a Philippino from Salinas, California. He was the nicest person, and unusually fair to everyone. He also had a black belt in Judo, as did I, and we both put on Judo instruction for the MP personnel. Our Operations Sergeant was a staff sergeant and, supposedly, a prison guard in Italy during World War II. We found that he had an IQ of 69 on record. He was a stupid ditz and always giving everyone trouble until he was transferred out. I was the only regular army enlisted personnel in the detachment other than the Operations Sergeant and Provost Sergeant.

Shortly after I arrived in the Philippines in December 1952, I was in town one night sitting at a bar-restaurant. I felt someone was looking at me continually. After looking around a few times I noticed a girl at a table, with a couple of other girls, looking at me. I turned around several times and she was still always looking at me, so I went over and introduced myself and found her name to be Lourdes Diangson The other girls left the table shortly but this lady continued to sit with me and we got acquainted. I found that she was sixteen years old and worked there as a waitress. She had been born in the Visayian Islands of the Philippines and lived through the Japanese occupation and later moved to Manila to live with her older sister. She then lived with a couple in Manila, a Mr. and Mrs. Gardner and their two daughters and baby son. Mr. Gardner was a Native Indian from Arizona. He had been a prisoner of the Japanese during the Bataan Death March. They had a beauty parlor and she helped doing nails and whatever was needed until she came to Cavite City. She came to Cavite City with her sister but her sister soon left and left her in the care of a motherly lady that ran a bar-restaurant called Jimmeys. She was very nice and I enjoyed her company. The next time I came into the restaurant she made a point to wait on me and would sit with me until another customer came in. Most of my MP duty was at night and the restaurant was not so busy during the day, therefore it was a normal time for me to visit. I tried to get her to let me escort her home to no avail. The restaurant owner, a woman, sent her home by a specific jeepney each night to protect her. In January, I met her boss and she seemed to like me and trust me. Everyone makes mistakes. One night in February I asked the young lady if she would go to the movies with me. She said on one condition. I would go to the movies and sit in a certain row. She and her girl friend would come to the movies and sit in the row behind me. It was a good movie, I guess, because they bothered me the whole show and left before I did. I never remembered the name of the movie. The last week in February this young lady finally let me escort her home as long as we would use her jeepney driver and he would bring me back into town. She lived in an apartment near the edge of town.

The week before this we had been sitting in the restaurant one afternoon and I had ordered lunch for both of us. She sat with me in a booth because it was her day off. I asked her to marry me and she excused herself and left the room. When she came back she said yes. She had asked the lady owner if it was OK, as I found out later. The owner helped us with the arrangements and gave us a big party after the church wedding. Since I was not a baptized Catholic we could not get married in a Catholic church. We had a protestant minister marry us and about fourteen years later we had a Catholic wedding. We originally married on March 6, 1953.

TOM AND LOURDES MORRING 1953

When we decided to get married I asked my commanding officer for a fifteen day leave. I then asked for his permission to get married. That was not army policy, and he said no, but said he was sure I would marry anyway. I got papers, from unknown sources, showing that I was a civilian visitor during the time I was on leave. I then got us a second story apartment near where Lourdes had been living and owned by her old landlord, who seemed to like me immensely. She gave us lots of extras, therefore I only had to buy us a new mahogany bed, with bamboo lining underneath, instead of springs. A very expensive marriage present to Lourdes and one that she loved immensely. I got permission to live off base, as long as I was always on base for all inspections, training, and whatever, and maintained my space, including bed, in my quarters. Life was again fun and great for the first time in four years. Lourdes got pregnant and was so happy, but we lost our first baby in early June. She was heartbroken but she marched on and got pregnant again in July.

Part of my MP duty was on a checkpoint coming into Cavite City from Manila. The U.S. embassy personnel hated to be stopped for identity before coming into town. They always tried to be belligerent, or thought they were superior to everyone else, and did not have to comply with rules. On several occasions they told the driver to not stop and I would draw my gun with all intentions to shoot the windows out of their vehicle if they did not stop. When the drivers saw the gun on them they would always stop, but it would be several yards beyond the check point. I would then make everyone get out of the car and stand with their hands on the car while I gave them a lecture. They later got even with me when Lourdes was trying to come to the U. S. The embassy personnel kept charging me uncalled for fees amounting to many thousands of dollars to allow my wife and child to come to the United States.

One day while on duty I got a call that a monkey was loose in the Post Exchange creating a ruckus. When I got there this monkey had a short leash on him and was very scared and mad because he was in unfamiliar surroundings. He saw me and came at me with his mouth open as if to bite me. Just as he got to my hand he turned his head away and I caught his leash. I was allowed to take him home as a pet since he had apparently been in captivity for some time. The monkey got along well with Lourdes and we kept him inside or tied up on a long leash to the clothes line. There was a friendly dog in the area and the dog would come over to meet the monkey and the monkey would massage the dogs back while hanging by his tail from the clothes line. If the monkey was inside when he heard the MP jeep bring me home he would run to the window and shake the window bars and scream until I came in and gave him a pat or a kind word. When Lourdes got pregnant the monkey did not like it if she hugged or kissed me. We knew that I was going to leave in a few months and we found a twelve year old house boy to stay with Lourdes and help her when I was gone. We gave the monkey to the houseboy.

I left the Philippines near the end of September 1953. My tour was up in November and I had to be processed for discharge. Lourdes could not come along but had to stay and be processed as an immigrant wife of a United States citizen.

Lourdes went to Manila to wave goodbye to me as we left. I was shipped back to Fort Knox, Kentucky for discharge. All other personnel that were being discharged were draftees and had to serve reserve status. I was the only regular army personnel being discharged. After three days I was processed, put on leave to complete my accumulated leave time, given discharge pay for the many months that I had not been paid, and a bus ticket back to Huntsville, Alabama. I had received ten dollars per month for most of my time overseas. I went to the Post Exchange and bought a new 30-30 Winchester rifle and a new set of wedding rings for Lourdes.

REBUILDING LIFE ALONE

After leaving the service, in November 1953, I went back to my old home place. I visited with my brother and his family for a few days. I had to get to work; therefore, I had to find what I wanted to do. I bought me a new GMC pickup truck, without a bed, and my brother and I immediately built a flat bed for the type of work I thought I might do. I started buying cows for resale and therefore drove a lot of country looking for cattle that I could buy right or trade. My brother, even though he could not see, was an expert at checking out cattle with his hands and helped me lots, in buying and loading the stock. It was a fun time but I could not make enough money since I was new to the trade.

I then decided to buy a D-4 Caterpillar tractor and a bush hog to clear new land and recondition scrub land for farmers. I got lots of work and did a lot for my brother. I also re-conditioned the river bottom land on our old home place, by taking out all of the hedgerows and slews that held mosquito water, and put it back into agriculture. I then found that I needed a bulldozer to do extra work. I bought an old RD-6 Caterpillar dozer and started clearing land and building drainage terraces for farmers. Over the years all farmers had been breaking or turning their land for crops to a depth of six to eight inches, therefore they had a shallow hardpan at that depth and plant roots would not go down and get moisture that was needed. I found a Case five pan disc breaking plow to pull behind the D-4 tractor and found that I could break ground, six feet wide and eighteen inches deep each time around the field. I could custom break land for four dollars per acre. I reconditioned my brothers' land and my old home place that year. It was a very dry year and we had better corn crops than most anyone. The next year I started breaking land, by the acre, for other farmers and had more work than I could do. I also bought another D-6 Caterpillar bulldozer for land clearing and drainage work.

I found a young man, just out of high school, that wanted a job. I hired him as a bull dozer operator (cat skinner) for minimum pay and found work clearing dead timber in the next county. The owner made and sold moonshine whiskey and I felt sure that I would get paid, because of the demand for good whiskey. It was a good job and would last for a long time. No other contractors would take the job; it was too dangerous, because dead timber would fall on the tractors and operator. The young man was a good worker and became a good friend and worked for me later in life, in California. Snakes of all types were prevalent on this site. He did not like the many snakes we found on the job. When we finished the job we did not get paid because the owner was caught by the federal authorities and put in jail for bootlegging. We lost over twenty thousand dollars on the job, which was a lot of money in those days.

People were always hunting on our farm property, especially the river bottom area, even though it was posted. I would use my rifle to drop a round near their feet to make them leave. Eventually the message got across the community that I was crazy enough to shoot someone and they should stay away from our property.

I needed a large truck to move my machinery and whatever else I could find to do. I found a used Chevrolet ten wheeler, twenty eight foot flat bed that would work well. I also put it to work hauling coal from Jasper, Alabama to local families in the county. During the season I would also haul baled cotton & cotton seed from the local gins to warehouses. It was a good workhorse. During the coal season, early fall, I would haul coal night and day and live on no-doze and coffee. I hired a young colored man, called Laughing Dan, to go with me sometimes. One time I got so sleepy that I told him to drive. He had never driven a truck, but this time he took over. I awoke with the truck engine screaming and we were doing ninety miles an hour down a steep grade. I immediately made him get over close to the door and I took over. We hit the bottom of the hill, with twenty eight tons of coal, doing one hundred miles an hour. When we finally got stopped, and wiped off the sweat, we got out and walked around to let the truck cool. He said, Master Tom, "I ain't never goin to drive a truck again". He still worked for me later at other work. He was too funny to let him get away. He always kept us laughing. One time we were cutting pine timber in our wooded area. Dan was working about two hundred yards away from the rest of us, cutting with a chain saw, and I heard him yell. About two minutes later I heard him yell again, about one half mile away, "*snake*". He had thrown down the chain saw and ran like hell. He would not ever go back into the woods.

One time Clyde and I were hauling the D-6 to Jackson County, Alabama up in the mountains, for another job. The tractor was so heavy and the curves so critical that on one curve the drive wheels touched the truck bed and locked up. The only way was to back up and try to straighten out the curve somewhat. Clyde got out of the truck on the passenger side and I told him to be careful, there was a long drop off the mountain on that side. He went around the truck in front and across the road. I backed the truck until the right rear trail wheels were off the cliff. I asked him to get back in and we would go. He said, "never mind, I will walk the rest of the way up the mountain". He had about a mile to walk, but he would not get back in the truck. He said, "You are crazy". When we got to the place to unload, there was no dirt bank or anything to back against to unload, so I just backed off the back end of the truck onto flat ground. The truck cab went away up in the air. He again said I was nuts. This was an ongoing favorite comment after that.

I was still gun shy when jets came over, after Korea. We were driving, slow, on the road one day when a jet came over very low. I bailed out of the truck, with Clyde still inside and the truck went into the ditch and scared him half to death. He didn't know what was going on, and after I explained, he asked that I never do that again. When we were together we would get us a pint or two of moonshine and drink quite a bit. One day when I was planting cotton on his farm, after we had been pretty drunk the night before, there was several comments made. It was a common joke, thereafter, that whoever plowed that cotton had to be drunk to plow it because the rows were so crooked. I also got polluted one night and side swiped a highway guard rail with the left side of my truck and did not know about it until one of Clyde's boys asked me about it the next morning. I had to re-track my trip to find where and what happened.

In fruit season I decided to go to Fort Valley, Georgia and get a load of peaches to haul to Tennessee or Kentucky for resale. Clyde went with me and of course had a pint of good moonshine for his nerves. He was well on his way and feeling no pain when we got to Fort Valley, Georgia. I saw a cop on the street corner and asked him for directions. Clyde asked him if he wanted a drink and showed him the bottle. Fortunately, the cop gave me directions and said nothing. I could have killed Clyde. For the next ten minutes I looked for a cop car to be behind us. We were lucky. The only peaches we could find were Hale or white meat peaches. I knew nothing about them but bought a truck load. When we got into Nashville they had already started to rot. They should have been kept refrigerated. We got rid of the peaches and went home broke. The life of a farmer, but I enjoyed the experience and the time with my brother.

Clyde and I seemed to like moonshine pretty good. It was a very good product that we bought from a specific bootlegger. In the wintertime we would sit around the fireplace, at Clyde's home, and tell jokes and have all of the family laughing. One time we were standing before the fire and telling all kinds of crude jokes and Clyde's wife said "that was just like brothers; drinking and spreading bullshit".

One day I met an old school buddy from prior years. He suggested we get a case of beer and five pounds of raw shrimp and just have an afternoon chat about old times. We talked, drank, and visited for several hours until the shrimp was gone. I had not seen him for about eight years. We had lots to catch up on about our travels and experiences.

I learned one lesson that I will never forget about machinery. One day as I was quitting work I turned the compression lever off on the RD-6 Caterpillar. Just as the engine was dying I decided I wanted to park the machine somewhere else. I quickly turned the compression lever back on and put the tractor in a forward gear. It went in reverse direction instead of forward. I backed the machine to where I wanted to park. I then put it in reverse gear and it went forward. I could not figure what I had done to cause the machine to go a different direction than I intended. I went to an old friend, Clifford Dean that had Caterpillars, and discussed the problem with him. He got a good laugh and told me it would be alright tomorrow. Since it was a three cylinder machine he said the motor kicked back when I released the compression and again put the compression back on and the engine had run backwards. It would run OK the next day. Live and learn. The old guys seem to have all the answers when you are young.

MY LIFE COMING TOGETHER

During the past year I had been continuously trying to get my wife, Lourdes and our new daughter, Oweni into the United States. I had sent Lourdes a new set of wedding rings, but the government would not let her have them without paying the cost of the rings in fees. Every time I sent papers or communication for her to come over, the government had to have some enormous fee, over twenty thousand dollars total. This even continued after our daughter was born. They finally communicated they would be on a ship to me in October. They would arrive in San Francisco and I would have to meet them. I left for San Francisco immediately. I called back home while on the trip west and was informed that they had been pulled off the shipment. They needed more papers and money to clear the port. At this point I was furious and I wrote the United States Embassy and the Philippine Attorney we had hired and told them I was broke. They would just have to keep them and support them. They showed these papers to Lourdes of course and she felt terrible. Again they asked for more funds and I repeated my answer. I was then told that they would be on the next ship and arrive on the President Cleveland Liner in early December.

I had to find some work and a place to stay until she arrived. I went to Los Angeles and spent my first night in my truck on the street. Next morning I was eating breakfast in an economical restaurant, Clifton's, and a gentleman sat down beside me and ordered coffee and then asked me if I was Thomas Morring. I was very surprised and answered yes. He told me he was my Uncle Bruce Morring. I had heard lots about him when I was growing up because my father was the only family member he ever communicated with. He told me that my mother had written him a letter and told him I was on my way to Los Angeles. How he knew what restaurant I would go to I will never know, it must have been God's directions. After we talked for a while he told me I could stay in a room above his garage. I told him I could not afford any rent, I was short of funds. We agreed that I would paint his rental house in return for rent. I only had five hundred dollars to continue to San Francisco and pick up Lourdes and Oweni. I had to make some money. I found, with my uncle's help, that the State of California was selling houses on the right of way for new freeways. They were auctioned at bid to be removed within thirty days. I went to the auctions, several times a day at different locations, and bought houses from five dollars to one hundred dollars. I sold them, sometimes within hours, to house movers, for one hundred dollars to five hundred dollars. Sometimes there were old cars left on the property by the past inhabitants. I would take these, in the middle of the night, and tow them to Griffith Park and dump them and get out of there as fast as I could. Other times I would take them across town and dump them in alleys. Sometimes I would have to demolish the house myself and I took the usable lumber and stored it at my uncle's place for future use. I made about fifteen hundred dollars plus my expenses while in Los Angeles. Some days I wouldn't even have money to eat, and would pick fruit off trees on the properties for food, or one time I found some onions and I ate several meals of onion soup cooked on a hot plate. I have only recently got to like onion soup again

During this stay, my uncle told me there was government land in the desert that you could homestead. We went to the Bureau of Land Management office in Los Angeles and found where the land areas were, and got the application papers. We then took a trip to the desert area near Desert Center, California to look at some of the land parcels that were available. We chose two one hundred and sixty acre parcels, one parcel between Desert Center and Blythe, and one north of Desert Center. We filed on these and were told we would get an answer in twelve to twenty four months.

In December, I went to San Francisco to meet Lourdes and Oweni when they arrived. I had never seen Oweni until the day the President Cleveland docked. I saw them both on the bridge and Oweni was in her mother's arms polishing the deck rail. She was eight months old. Lourdes looked very thin and weak. When they debarked they had to go through customs and I was waiting beside the fence for them. A customs supervisor came to me from inside the fence and asked if I was Mr. Morring. He told me to follow the fence to the gate and meet him there. At the gate he told me to follow him. He took me to meet Lourdes and Oweni, told me to take their bags and follow him. He took us around customs and told me to meet customs, with my wife and daughter, at a designated customs office the next day. When we got outside old friends of Lourdes, Bill and Gloria Gardner, met us and told us to follow them to their home, but we decided to go to a hotel for our first night together in sixteen months. We were then informed that they had been held up because Lourdes had blood type "A-Positive". After our customs clearance we went to Gardeners home for a couple of days. We then returned to Los Angeles and picked up my belongings and left for Alabama on Christmas Eve.

Since I was running short of funds we drove non stop twenty three hundred miles to our new home. Lourdes and Oweni slept most of the way except when we stopped to eat or use a rest room. The trip from Los Angeles to Huntsville, Alabama took twenty seven hours. I slept for two days after that.

The attitude in the south was very prejudiced at that time, and my wife was not looked upon favorably by anyone but my brothers' family. My mother came home in a few days and tried to be civil but it was visibly clear that there was resentment because I had married a foreign wife. We therefore bought a small trailer home and set it up on the front part of the old home property. My father had left the property to me at my mother's death, but she had asked me to deed my interest to her in case something happened to me, while I was in the service. I still claimed that I had an interest in the farm but she said that I did not, since I had deeded it to her. I began making long term plans for us a home but I had no cash left, only machinery. I went back to work farming, earth moving, trucking, and whatever I could, to make money. I was working long hard hours and was not at home like I would like to have been. Clyde still helped as much as possible and we did some farming together. I also enrolled in machinist trade school, under the G.I. Bill, near Decatur, Alabama at night.

Lourdes got pregnant again. The pregnancy and being alone so much was very hard on her so soon after her waiting so long to come home from the Philippines. She was also critical of Clyde and I drinking moonshine so much. She was right, but I wouldn't quit. I felt I needed some relief from working so much. One night, in early October on my way home from night school, I was met head on, on my side of the road, by another driver, in a horrendous auto accident. The other driver was killed instantly, and determined to have been drunk, and I was taken to the hospital in Huntsville with concussion, many cuts, broken knee and ankle, and unconscious for a long, long time. Clyde's family would bring Lourdes to see me when they could during the day and Clyde would stay with me at night for a long time. I do not know how Lourdes kept her sanity with me gone, her five months pregnant, and the indecision as what she would do if I did not recover. However, one morning when Clyde was there, it seemed as if someone raised the shades in the room and I was awake. I did not know where I was, or why I was there. Clyde immediately told me what was what and showed me a newspaper clipping of the accident. My left knee and ankle had been crushed and they had removed the kneecap and had my leg in a cast to my hip. They found the ankle had been crushed too late to do anything with it. A shard of glass had pierced my left eye but did not do major injury. Soon I got out of the hospital and a few days later our son Thomas Norberto Morring was born. He was a big baby, weighing almost ten pounds. It was very hard for Lourdes the next several months with a new baby, Oweni, and me in crutches.

During my stay in the hospital the banker that held mortgages on most of my equipment foreclosed, bought the equipment at less than half of what it was worth, and took it to his farm for his own use. We had crops to plant and therefore I was forced to borrow my brothers' tractor to put in crops. Shortly thereafter I collected some money that had been owed to me and bought an Oliver 70 farm tractor. I had a tenant farmer that did all of the work with the help of my brother in starting new crops. I still had no transportation and had to hitch hike ten miles, on crutches, to the doctor when I had to go. I would be hitch hiking on the road near home and people that owed me money would pass, look the other way when they passed, and not even give me a ride. This embittered me greatly. I have never forgotten this, but I am sure they did, because they never paid me. Soon I accumulated enough money to buy a used Ford military jeep. I could drive it OK because I could shift gears without using the clutch. It was a real work horse. When we gathered corn that fall Clyde found us a one row mechanical corn picker. I used his tractor because it had a hand clutch. I, while standing up, picked a couple hundred acres of corn with that tractor and corn picker and hauled the corn in a trailer to the grainery with the jeep, while in the leg cast. What a year.

Lourdes and the children were doing OK but Thomas was about to eat her up. He wanted to nurse all of the time. One night when we were coming home from Clyde's we were hit broadside as we crossed the highway. Thomas was thrown out, Oweni got a bad cut on her forehead, Lourdes head hit mine and she was unconscious. Lourdes and Oweni were taken to the hospital. Clyde's wife took Thomas home, and Oweni also, when she was released. Lourdes had a severe concussion and did not know me for several days. The nurses caught her trying to get out the window in the hospital. On investigation it was found the driver did not have his lights on and was driving by the moonlight because his generator was out of order. Of course he had no insurance. When Lourdes got out of the hospital she complained with her left arm and head hurting. She had problems with it even ten years later.

We were notified shortly thereafter that one homestead entry in California had been accepted and we had two years to move on the property, build a house, drill a well, and cultivate it. We immediately got ready to leave Alabama and go to California. We sold everything we could, bought us a Pontiac sedan with automatic transmission, installed trailer hitch and Clyde and I built a small trailer, with a wooden tongue, to haul personal goods to California. Since I had just had the fifth operation on my knee, three days before we left, I could only drive approximately one hundred miles and had to stop and rest. The trip took five days and it was hell. The trailer broke down in Oklahoma and a nice gentleman in a shop fixed it and would not even let us pay him. He stated it looked like we had enough trouble and needed some help. We thanked him very much and proceeded on our way to California.

EARLY YEARS IN CALIFORNIA

When we got to Los Angeles we stayed in my Uncle Bruce's garage apartment while I got things ready to move to the desert. I found a very used twenty one foot house trailer and towed it to the desert site. On the way out of Los Angeles we were stopped by a cop because we were driving too slow on the freeway. I was driving forty five miles an hour because the trailer tires were old. I therefore increased speed up to sixty miles an hour till we got out of Los Angeles area. We made the trip OK, set up the trailer, and returned to LA.

Uncle Bruce and I purchased a 1955 Chevrolet truck from Felix Chevrolet for Seven Hundred dollars. The truck was new, but two years old. For the next several days we hauled the surplus lumber, one hundred ninety three miles to the desert, making one round trip each day, and stored the lumber where we were going to build a house. I was getting pretty tired from the round trips, driving six hours, each day, plus loading and unloading and was starting to go to sleep driving on the road in the early morning hours. Uncle Bruce and I were coming from Los Angeles one day and I went to sleep east of Indio, near Cactus City, when Uncle Bruce yelled at me just before I was about to rear end a semi truck. Uncle Bruce suggested, and we then decided to move to the desert into the trailer and start building. It was July and hot as hell in the desert (120+ degrees F.) and we had no electricity, generator, cooler or any way to keep cool. I slept in the trailer at night, on the floor by the door, with the door open, and listened to the snakes crawl and the coyotes walk around in search of food, and Lourdes and the children got by somehow sleeping in the interior. We needed a generator badly. It had been almost two years since I had been able to work.

I went to Desert Center and tried to get a job pumping gas or anything. I was still cripple from the surgery, and my left leg was wired stiff at the knee. I applied for a job at the best looking service station and was turned down. I applied at the Chevron Truck Stop and was hired at one dollar per hour plus commission for changing truck tires or lubrication jobs. Gasoline was twenty five cents per gallon at that time. After a couple of weeks, I was working twelve to sixteen hours per day and my wife and children were alone eighteen miles East in the desert. One day there was a dust storm in their area and a stranger brought them to me at the truck stop. They were scared to death because the only dust storm they had seen was in the movies. The truck stop owner rented us a house to stay in and we moved to Desert Center and set up better living quarters for my family. Approximately one week later the other attendant at the truck stop was fired and I had it all by myself for the next three days until another body was hired. Lourdes would bring the children to the station at night and watch while I took naps. When customers would come in she would wake me up. They would sleep in the daytime.

In December, Lourdes got pregnant again. I was promoted to manager of the truck stop and things got a little easier. The young man that I had hired as cat skinner called and wanted to come to California. I told him I would hire him as station attendant and I would let him stay with us for a while in one of the little rooms in our house. This helped a lot to have someone that I could depend on at the station part of the day. This gave me some spare time to work on our house at the ranch, which we had named El Rancho Rebelde, (the rebelling ranch).

There was one comical occurrence at home at dinnertime when I was teasing Lourdes. I was sitting at the dinner table with our guest when Lourdes had enough. She told me to quit teasing and I just laughed at kept at it. She threw a fork across the table at me and it stuck in my chin. I just laughed harder with the fork in my chin and the guest jumped back and started to get up. I told him everything was OK and we went ahead with eating. Lourdes broke up crying and I told her I was so sorry. I had not intended to tease her to this point. I tried to never do that again. After all it might be dangerous.

One night that fall we spent one night in the trailer doing some work. I heard a noise in the night and I went outside to see what was happening. I had been carrying a 30-30 Winchester in my truck everywhere I went for the whole time I was in the desert. I saw two men, or older boys, breaking boards at our house site. I immediately hollered at them and got my gun and fired at their car, as they left. Some months later I found the car. It belonged to the business manager of the community where I was working.

The car had two bullet holes in the chassis, but the owner denied that he knew anything about the incident. I had reported the incident to the Sheriff's office but they did nothing but take the report.

At a later date I went to the ranch one day to check and found our beginning home burned completely up. Someone had done a good job. Again the Sheriff's office did nothing except take the report. The fellow employees at Desert Center wanted to take up a collection of money and supplies for us. They were told by the management that if they gave us any help they would be fired. From this time on I was a loose cannon just waiting for someone to kill or beat to death. Some months later I arrived at the ranch one day and a sheep herder was parked near the house site and was looking around the trailer. I got out of my truck, rifle in hand, and asked him what he was doing. He stated he was just looking around. I asked him what he had in the trunk of his car. He said nothing. I asked him to open the trunk, but he refused. I took the rifle and blew the lock out of his trunk and opened it. There was one of my five gallon cans in the trunk. I took the can and gave him three minutes to get off the property or I would shoot him. He left very quickly. A week later my family and I were going the fifty miles to Blythe to shop. We liked to stop at a little restaurant about five miles from the Blythe Airport and have something cold to drink since the desert was so hot. The ladies there told us that a sheepherder had stopped by and told them there was a crazy man out in the desert. He said the guy had tried to kill him. He was quitting and leaving California. He was herding sheep for a rancher in Blythe. I found that he just left the sheep and left California.

I began planning to build a new house on the ranch. I started working at night at the service station and in the mornings I would go, one hundred twenty five miles to Riverside and get a pickup truck load of lumber and building materials and take to the ranch. I did this for about a month. During this time I hired a contractor, Willie Summers, who came to Desert Center most every year during the wintertime to work. His wife, Squeky Summers, worked in the café as a waitress. Willie poured my footings and floor for the new house and installed the walls. I also built us an outhouse for use until we could do better.

In July 1958, while changing a truck tire, for a customer, a lug bolt broke while I was using a long pipe cheater to loosen the nut. I fell and tore my left knee apart where it had been wired together. I had to go to the hospital and have surgery. They removed about a pint of sutures, broken bones, and cartilage from my knee. The doctor, of Indian heritage, told me that if I would wait until he had left the room, I should pull the left ankle up and touch my rear end. If I would do that regularly, I would walk out of the hospital without the aid of crutches. It had been wired together about three years, but I did what he instructed and screamed loud enough to be heard the fifty miles in Desert Center. The knee has been operating satisfactorily, but painfully, ever since.

In August of 1958 our son Benjamin Thomas Morring, III was born. Lourdes went into labor, every three minutes in Desert Center. My friend let me borrow his Oldsmobile sedan to take her to the hospital in Indio. I could not drive my truck because of my leg and its manual clutch for shifting. On the way to the hospital we passed a CHP patrol car going the other way. He observed my speed and tried to catch me. He caught me in the hospital just as our son was born. He wanted to know what I was driving and wanted to see it. He did not give me a ticket. I had made the fifty mile trip in twenty seven minutes. The Oldsmobile had been built for stock car racing and ran, even in the summertime in the desert, without a fan,. It was a very fast car.

After Ben's birth, Lourdes got a part time job cleaning the motel in the town. She would move Ben's crib next to my bed, since I was working at night, and he would climb out of his crib and ride horsey on my stomach while I slept. Lourdes would find him there when she, Tom and Oweni would come back home from her work.

While my knee recuperated I was given the job as cashier in the towns' restaurant. After I was able to go back to work I was again promoted to delivering fuel and oils to contractors, Kaiser Steel, and Metropolitan Water District plants in the desert for the Chevron Oil Distributor. This kept me busy ten hours per day, usually. I would have Saturday and Sundays off to work on my house. One week I noticed our outhouse was missing. I started looking at every desert habitat location for it. I found it at a ranch between our house site and Desert Center. I backed my truck up to it, taking my rifle as I got out of the truck, and started to load it. Two guys came out of a trailer on the land. When they observed me with the rifle they went back inside. I loaded the outhouse and took it home. I also got a contractor to drill me a six hundred twenty foot deep water well. We got good water. I was next able to find me a propane powered, ten kilowatt, generator for power. Then I found a well pump and a V-4 Wisconsin engine for pump power. I also installed a one thousand gallon storage tank on stilts for water pressure. I was now ready to get the house built. We already had the floor poured and the side walls, windows, and doors up. We moved into our new house before the rafters or the roof was put on. Starlight nights. We had it equipped with propane refrigerator and stove for cooking.

During the months prior I had bought a Caterpillar crawler tractor for clearing purposes. There were many new water wells being drilled on the land around Desert Center and the drilling rigs were always getting stuck in the sand. I rented my tractor to most of them to pull their drilling rigs and water trucks to the drilling sights. It got a good workout and I made a considerable amount of money on this venture.

I got a job at Kaiser Steel as a diesel mechanic and welder in January 1960. I was scheduled to work eight hours per day. Shortly after I started they had me working on one hundred ton trucks, locomotives, and drilling rigs on the mountain. They liked my work and I was selected to work overtime considerably. The pay was $4.35 per hour, time and a half for overtime, and double time on weekends and holidays. The money part was good but I was working myself to death and my family was alone so much. My weight went from one hundred sixty five to one hundred thirty five pounds in the nine months. I also had to drive fifty miles per day to work. Whenever I was off work I had to keep water pumped and do building on the house that I could. I finally was able to hire an individual contractor to finish up the house. In about June that year Kaiser had a decrease in production and cut everyone off overtime. It was immediately learned that I had experience as a Caterpillar tractor mechanic and I was asked to work twelve hour shifts seven day per week during the cutback. This was again good for my budget since the cutback.

In September, 1960 I came home one evening and the old man that owned most of Desert Center was sitting in his car at my house. He wanted to talk to me about working for him again. He said he was going to fire his business manager since he had caught him stealing and was offering me the job. He would provide us a house to live in with all utilities paid, all meals for me at the restaurant free if I wanted, free fuel for my truck, and five hundred per month for a two year contract. I was on duty twenty four hours per day, seven days per week but could work the daily hours I was needed. This was a good deal because Oweni was ready to go to school and school was five hundred yards away from home. The house that was supplied was built with only the outside siding. The inside was unfinished, without windows but there were screens, over openings, covered with solid wood shutters, to close in case of rain or excess wind. It had been built by one of Metropolitan Water District's contractors for his use many years before.

The management job was operating the truck stop, restaurant, motel, wholesale oil delivery plant, repair garage, towing service, grocery store, and about twenty five rental houses. Commercial electric power was new to the area and there were quite a few power outages. The town owned two, one hundred kilowatt, generators that had been used for power for years. We had to maintain these in usable condition for such outages. I had my own office, a bookkeeper, and about thirty five employees at all times. If there was a problem at night I was called to solve the problem, because the Sheriff had to come all the way from Blythe, a fifty mile trip. Whenever I went out at night I always carried a hand gun on me. There was one time I remember that the dishwasher woke me up at night and said a man was causing a disturbance in the restaurant. When I got there the man was very belligerent and would not leave. He decided he was going to fight me. I then hit him in the head with my pistol and threw his body out the door. He awoke in a few minutes, got in his car, and left driving drunk. There was a problem one other time, near midnight, with an employee and his wife who lived in one of the rentals. I went there with my gun and gave them thirty minutes to move out of the house and leave town or I was going to shoot someone. When I was challenged by the husband I shot a hole in the floor near his foot. They were gone within twenty minutes.

Lots of time we would not have a mechanic available for tow truck service and I would have to go out, night or day. I got a call one night to pick up a vehicle about twenty miles east of Desert Center. When I got to the vehicle, a Buick Roadmaster, it had to be towed since the engine had locked up. There were two men and a woman in the car. I put them in the cab with me and hauled the car to the Desert Center garage. The men said they would take the next bus to Los Angeles and have the car picked up. About three days later an FBI agent wanted to see me. He told me they had murdered a postmaster in New Mexico, a service station owner in Arizona, and were very dangerous. He wanted all the information I could give him and he would have their car towed to a storage place. He said I was very lucky, especially since I had a gun on me that night. The job never had a dull moment, day or night.

The job had its comical moments also. We usually had thirty or thirty five employees on payroll. The attrition of personnel was great. Possible employees were always looking for jobs. It seems most of the applicants thought they could do everything, cook, waitress, store keeper, service station operator or whatever. If they told me this, I would not hire them.

If they had a specialty I usually would give them a try. Lots of them were alcoholics and on days off would go into town somewhere, get drunk and locked up in jail. On one occasion I remember a young man, Johnny Dollar, a part Indian, that this happened to several times. When he got out of jail he would come back. One time on payday I tried to get him to stay and not go to town. He said he had to get a haircut. I told him I would give him a haircut for free. He agreed and I took him to the garage and cut his hair. That was the last time he would let me do that. He told me a bit of his childhood while I was cutting his hair. He said he and a school friend went home with another friend one day. At breakfast the next morning they had biscuits and gravy. He asked his friend "pass me the drease," his friend replied, "you mean the dravy". He was a real character to know and we became friends, to a point.

During this time I had a very special lady, Ethel Rowe, as a friend and bookkeeper. She was an excellent person in all respects and she and Lourdes had a good time together, even though there was approximately twenty years difference in age. I was busy in the office one day and was waiting on someone at the office window when the telephone rang. It was for me and while on the phone, waiting on a customer at the window, the intercom from the garage called me, and then a second phone rang. I took care of all of these at once. Ms. Rowe made several comments later that she had never seen anyone take care of this many things at one time.

In late 1960, when I was working as manager, the Army Demolition Crew came to Desert Center and wanted to rent the motel and a couple of rental houses for a couple of months. Some old munitions had been unearthed in the land clearing that was being done for farming and they were going to comb the area from Blythe to Indio and From Desert Center to Needles to recover some of the products left by the U.S. Army during training in World War II. This was necessary to prevent accidents from getting someone hurt by old explosive materials.

Shortly thereafter in 1961, Harold Geisener, an employee of the federal government came by and wanted a motel room for a couple of months. He was making a geological survey of the water in the basin between Indio and Blythe and documenting all water wells in the area. He asked for my assistance in locating these wells because it was determined that I had great knowledge of their whereabouts. I gave him all the information that I could and helped him locate many water wells that had been left abandoned. He sent me an original of his report after he had finished. I still have this report and some added information since that time. I am told the State of

California no longer has a copy of this report. I have had five water wells drilled in the area myself.

The report indicated a good quantity of water in the underground basin. There had been, and continue to be, reports of no water or insufficient water in the area and reports of detrimental contents, that are usually untrue.

When I had been working at the truck stop, a gentlemen, and well driller, named Howard Brown, came by and introduced himself as a promoter. He had acquired a desert land entry on three hundred twenty acres three miles north of Desert Center on the Parker-Rice Highway. We became good friends and eventually did some farming together on his acreage. He rented some equipment from me and eventually bought a Ferguson tractor and a Caterpillar tractor from me. When I got to be manager of Desert Center he would come to the restaurant each morning and have coffee while he was waiting for the Post Office to open. We usually had coffee together and talked about things. On one occasion his car was parked in front of the restaurant and his bulldog was sitting behind the steering wheel with his front legs over it. At first I thought Howard was sitting in his car. As I went around the car I saw the illusion. When I went inside I told Howard what I saw and told him what I had first thought. We had a big laugh about this. A short time thereafter his bulldog got killed by a badger on his ranch.

The company made money under my management but the cantankerous old man was hard to work for. He wanted to be in my face four of five hours per day five days per week telling him what was going on in detail. After much argument about wasting my time he decided I needed an assistant and he hired a local man which I did not like. My two year contract was almost over and I had his accountant make an audit of the books. He said everything was in order. I asked the old man and his nurse to come to the office the next day for the audit report. After the accountant had made his report the old man wanted to give a long dialogue about what should be done and introduce the new assistant to the accountant. I stopped him immediately and told him the next day was my last day. I had finished my two year contract. He tried to threaten me but I had just provided him with a current audit report and I told him if I heard any threats to my character he would be sued to the maximum. That was the last I heard from him.

Some short months later he hired a man from Palm Desert, California to take charge of all of his businesses and he hired a manager. The manager used to be an official from American Can Company. The new manager closed most of the rental houses and had them torn down, closed the motel, truck stop, garage, tow service, Chevron bulk oil distributorship, and decreased the amount of groceries in the store. Shortly thereafter the old man made a deal with his son that owned a Texaco station in town, to take over the complete business.

When I left management of the businesses I already had a job waiting for me at Metropolitan Water District, Hayfield Station. We moved into one of their houses and I went to work as a utility man. The district provided transportation for the school students to Eagle Mountain High School. About a year later I was promoted to mechanic to work on vehicles, air conditioning, or whatever. About six months later I was promoted to plant machinist, after they found I had machinist training. At this location everyone helped at whatever was needed when you had time from your own job assignment. Sometimes helping electricians, overhaul the enormous electric pumps, welding, cleaning, or whatever. There were 6,300 volt electrical power conduits running from the switch yards to the pump station. These conduits were lead encased and laid in troughs. The heat would make these conduits crawl back and forth as temperatures change. The conduits were oil filled and we found one of them leaking one time. I volunteered to seal the leak with a torch and everyone said they would blow up. After a couple of weeks discussion I was allowed to try. Everyone left the area because they knew tragedy was going to happen. I fixed the leak without any trouble and was told I was nuts. They said if it were to short out and explode, there would not be even a greasy spot left behind.

The beams above the large electric motors were about forty feet up from the floor of the main building. Twice yearly my job was to climb upon these beams and clean them using the assistance of a twenty ton crane mounted nearby for assistance. Everyone else always seemed too busy to help. I believe it was because it was so high up from the floor. They did not like this height. After five years working there I got an excellent job evaluation and everyone, but me, got a raise. I challenged why I had not gotten a raise. The answer was that since I had bought a property in Desert Center and built a store and duplex it was determined that I did not need the money. I gave my thirty day notice to quit and did so. During the past two years I had taken tests to get certification with American Water Works Association as a public water works operator. There were four grades of operator and I had gotten the highest certification.

During the years that I was working at Desert Center we had met a nice older couple from an area known as Aztec Wells that is located south east of Desert Center. Bill and Maude Seidel was an unusual couple. Mr. Seidel was a German emigrant that had spent his lifetime working on ships and dredging the beaches and rivers for better access or channeling. Mrs. Seidel was originally from the eastern part of the United States. They had retired on a mining claim in Aztec Wells about six miles southeast of Desert Center. They were a nice and friendly couple and we had many visits with them at their home. They had bought six and a half acres, adjoining the Ragsdale property in Desert Center. They finally agreed to sell it to us, in two parcels, with payments over five years. The one acre parcel was paid in full. The balance was to be paid over five years. We paid them off after three years and Mrs. Seidel was very unhappy that we paid it off early. We immediately began plans for building on the property.

We developed plans for duplexes, a small store building that we could convert to a rental unit if the store failed, and a motel. We would name the store Chuckwalla Market. I derived the name from the Chuckwalla lizard, a slow growing, vegetarian, and very stable animal that lives to an old age. This is the way I envisioned our market growing. The valley area was known as Chuckawalla Valley, therefore I did not want the conflict with that name. There are lots of Chuckwalla lizards in the area.

During the third year that I had worked with MWD, I had made contact with a contractor that had built some nice homes for them. This contractor also built shells of buildings for the owners to finish themselves. I made a contract with them to build a duplex and a single, twenty four by twenty four foot, rental unit that I could modify into a store building and if the store was a failure I could use it as a rental dwelling unit. The cost of the shells and finishing materials, for both buildings was less than nine thousand dollars. I, of course, had to build septic tanks with leach fields for both units and pipe in water supplies. We did not have a well, but I made a deal with a local rancher friend of mine for water. I had to haul water and pump into my storage tank and pressure system. I worked on the store building first and had it ready to occupy as a store on March 1, 1965. I worked for MWD twenty one days and had five days off regularly. I did the building construction on my days off, usually working sixteen hours per day. I had to do the electrical installation, install fiberglass insulation, drywall, internal plumbing, flooring, and painting. When I got ready for the power to be hooked up, Southern California Edison refused to supply me power because I did not have a previous contract with the power company that had installed the power lines across my property. SCE had purchased the company that had installed the power lines. I brought in the generator from the ranch and opened anyway and responded to SCE, in writing, that if I did not have power I would buy a new Caterpillar generator and sue them for my cost and damages. They would have to remove the power line off my property. Two days later, on a Friday evening, after 5:00 PM, the SCE installation crew arrived and hooked up my power.

I had gotten a beer and wine license allotted from the state, some couple of months earlier. We opened the store on March 1, 1965 with a soda pop cooler for beer and soda pop, an old freezer, a potato chip and candy rack, and a shelf for bread and cookies. Our total sales the first day was about one hundred dollars. I knew the beer and wine would bring the business because there was none in Desert Center, or nearby. At the end of March we were taking in about five hundred dollars per day. The weather turned off very hot and I had to buy and install air conditioning the last day of March. This destroyed our budget but we survived. We continually added more shelves, equipment, supplies, and groceries thereafter. Business was growing well and we had a good supply of customers because we had started getting the home bound Kaiser Steel workers that commuted from Indio, Blythe, Twenty Nine Palms and outside areas. We started staying open from 7:00 AM to 9:00 PM, seven days per week to accommodate the shift changes from Kaiser. We had Lourdes and one employee that would work shifts daily.

Lourdes, who spent most of the time in the store, loved children. The school bus would stop on its way to games or other trips and the students would come in to get snacks and soda pop. If they were short of funds, or did not have any funds, Lourdes would give them the snacks they wanted and wish them well. Sometimes people would come through the area and come into the store and ask for a handout. Lourdes would ask if there were children or family in their car. If they said yes, she would ask for the children and family to come in and she would give them food to eat and drink, but no cash handouts or beer to anyone. If an older man would come in, usually with a bad attitude and ask, "where is the beer", she would ask him if he was old enough, and get him laughing. He would leave in a good mood.

We did not have any protection for our store clerks in case someone tried to commit robbery on us. I applied for, and purchased a thirty eight caliber pistol to be kept at the store for the ladies protection because the nearest law enforcement was fifty miles away. A week later the Sheriff's office confiscated the weapon from us because I had been charged and sentenced for aggravated assault while in the army, even though the charge was exonerated. We then provided the store with a bayonet I bought from Army Surplus. This was OK according to the sheriff. However, about five years later the Blythe Sheriff Station Commander, which I had known for a long time, asked me what kind of protection we had for the store personnel. Lourdes had a .32 Caliber pistol she had gotten somewhere, behind the cash register for protection, and I showed it to him. He said to get rid of that thing and get a real gun, a .357 caliber magnum pistol, and if anyone tried to rob us to use it and make sure the body was inside the store. I shortly thereafter bought a .357 caliber magnum pistol from a private party and I still have it. I eventually did quite a few trips of flying for the Sheriff's Department, for free.

After I finished working for MWD we decided to keep the store open from 7:00 AM to midnight daily. I would open the store and Lourdes would come in later. Mrs. Murphy worked an eight hour shift, and I would close up. After about a year I got a job as a core drillers' helper, drilling for iron ore, with Continental Drilling Company at the Kaiser Steel Mine. After about a month I was promoted to driller. There was a very demanding schedule because the drilling company got paid by the foot drilled. If the driller didn't get the footage he would be looking for a job. We were drilling at a forty five degree incline and retrieving the cores. Sometimes we would have to pull the tools out of the hole four or five times a day. We were drilling from 0 to 2500 foot depths. During the summertime most of us did not wear shirts because it was so hot. The drilling sites were set up on poles as a tripod with pulley and cable in the center with the diesel power unit with gear head set at the angle to be drilled and a second story platform for the helper to pull the columns out of the way as they came out of the hole, or to go in as needed. We finished our contract after about a year and the company offered me the opportunity to continue but go to Yucca Valley and drill for gold. I had to drive about two hundred miles per day and work twelve hours. After we finished the gold drilling, the job in the desert was done, and I was offered a job on an oil drilling rig north of Ventura, California. I declined this job because I was needed at home to work near the store and home.

This was early 1968 and I was notified that Riverside County Service Area (CSA 51) wanted someone with some credentials to work as Public Works Superintendant. When I interviewed it was determined that I had the necessary qualification and I got the job. Starting pay was fourteen hundred fifty dollars per month and a vehicle and fuel was supplied. The job was only one mile from my home. The CSA manager was a prior Kaiser Steel mine superintendant and an excellent person to work with. My duties included, inspection, approving construction of, maintaining or seeing maintained; the water purification facility, sewer facility, all water and sewer lines, all public buildings and equipment, pump stations both irrigation and domestic, reading and servicing all water meters and backflow devices, starting and designing the operation for a water de-fluoridation plant, caring for the operation and maintenance of all golf course equipment, bookkeeping and budgeting for the same. I was also allowed and encouraged, with approval, to go to more schooling in any and all of these subjects to improve my knowledge at public expense.

One of my first trips was to go to backflow testing and certification school in Newport Beach. I went to a sewer treatment school in Fresno and Riverside. I went to water treatment plants in Lancaster, Palmdale, and Palm Springs. I then went to San Diego to take the state exam for Sanitary Engineer. After finishing the six hour test I was sure I had failed and told Lourdes it was a bad day. The family had gone with me and waited all day for me in the car and shopping near the hotel where the test was held. About five days later I got the results and I had passed the engineering exam. I was relieved because I had studied for several months to take the exam. One of my next schools was a chemical corrosion school held at USC. I had gotten a room there, to sleep in, for the three day school. One of the students at the school was a MWD superintendant that I knew. He could not believe that I was at the school for that class since I had been only an employee of MWD, and not an engineer. Lourdes and the children were coming in to the area for the night and I had gotten a motel room for us. I found that the MWD gentleman did not have a place to stay and I told him he could use my room. He could not believe I would do this since he was one of the persons that turned down my raise with MWD.

We had been working on the water treatment plant for approximately one and a half years to remove fluoride to the acceptable level of 1.5 Parts Per Million maximum and 0.8 PPM average. This was the levels determined to be acceptable by the federal government to prevent tooth damage to children and adults. The natural water had approximately 12.0 PPM Fluoride. It was impossible to reach these levels with the way the water treatment plant had been designed. The design engineers, a Los Angeles firm, had spent several months, at the facility with me, trying to get it to work. The plant was designed according to a test facility in Bartlett, Texas that was supposed to be working according to the federal government.

Kaiser Engineers, a division of Kaiser Operations then recommended an engineer, James Strong, from San Francisco to examine the plant operation. His determination, after several weeks, was that the plant would never operate properly the way it was designed. It was decided that he and I would go to Bartlett, Texas and review that plants operation. We flew to Austin, Texas and rented a car to travel to Bartlett. We went to Bartlett to review what was in the town and to find a place to stay. There were no hotels or motels to be found. We did find a restaurant there and had lunch. We were viewed with suspicion by the people in the restaurant because we were definitely strangers. We got a hotel in a nearby town for five days. The next day we went to Bartlett and introduced ourselves to the city staff and confirmed our permission to review their water treatment plant. That day, about noon, the City Manager came over to the plant and instructed us that we should not review things too closely. They had reported their facts to the federal government and that should be sufficient for anyone. We explained our problem and stated we were trying to find what our problem was. He insisted that we confine our test to what our problem was. He was a born Georgia native, and was a very large, fat man and a typical politician in a small town. We went to lunch afterwards and tried to talk to some local residents. They again viewed us with suspicion and told us nothing of value except that they take care of their own business. We reviewed the records from the water plant and some things did not make sense. We asked what they did with the effluent from the treatment process. They said they thought it went to the river. One day, late in the evening, we went to the river and took a sample where the effluent was discharged. It was extremely high in fluoride content. It was definitely an illegal discharge into public waterways. We were told the next morning that we had been observed taking the sample and that people were known to have disappeared when they got too nosey. We left that evening and finished our trip. It was evident the plant had never worked and the records had been rigged to get the grant from the federal government. It was decided that we would write our report when we got back and determine what action we must take to make our plant work successfully. We went back to Austin and the engineer flew home to San Francisco and I flew to Palm Springs. On the flight home I studied the Bartlett notes and some bright light in my head made me design a method I thought might work. The notes had led me to believe the chemical contents of the water was different, therefore we needed a different chemical process to remove the fluoride. I wrote a test process from my prior notes while on the plane.

When I got back to CSA 51, I built a pilot test water purification station and started running test operations until I got one that would work repeatedly to the same specifications. I documented all the tests and information. I then conferred with the engineer I had been working with and he came back and spent a couple of weeks and recommended we make the necessary changes to the water plant to make it work as my test had shown. The major changes were to substitute sulphuric acid for hydrochloric acid. Since sulphuric acid is more aggressive we had to line our acid tanks for storage. It took less sulphuric acid to run the regeneration process and remove the fluoride from the activated alumna media in the water purification tanks, but sulphuric acid was more expensive. The process was however duplicated each time successfully and the system was accepted by the Riverside County Health Department and the State of California Public Health.

During this time I had taken a couple days trip to Los Angeles to confer with the State Health Department. During this time we had the 1971 earthquake that did so much damage in Los Angeles and immediate area. I had spent the night at the Hilton Hotel. When the quake started I tumbled out of bed and right to the window. People were running out of the hotel, yet they were immediately obstructed from my view by the movement of the hotel. When the shaking stopped I decided I needed a shower because I heard water running. I had forgotten that my room was next to the elevator shaft. A water line had broken above my floor and the water was running down from that break. I was still able to take a shower with less water pressure. When I went out I had to walk down three floors to the garage. I found a large slab of concrete had fallen next to my car; therefore I moved my car out on the street and checked out. I tried to call home but could not get through. I finished my work at the state lab and returned home.

In developing the continuity of the water plant I was required to sometimes work in the middle of the night. On one occasion I was, inside the building, making some test on a water analysis and had a pipette of sulphuric acid up to my mouth when I felt a tapping on the side of my right foot. I looked down and a small side winder (rattle snake) had come into the building under the door and apparently felt the heat of my foot and was rattling against my foot. I jumped up and stomped him to death. I then noticed that I had sucked the acid into my mouth. My guns were burning severely. I washed my mouth out with water many times and it quit burning. Approximately a year later I had to go to the dentist and found that I was going to lose all of my front teeth because of the infection. They were removed and replaced with a bridge.

Shortly thereafter I was hit in the back of the head by a golf ball while working on an irrigation time clock on the edge of the golf course. The golfer came over and asked, "Are you all right". Even though I was knocked to my knees, I felt OK. I finished with the time clock and decided to go home. I felt like I was partially drunk. I was stopped by a Sheriff deputy, one mile way from home. He said I was driving erratic. I told him what had happened and he followed me home. I went to a doctor the next day and was sent to Riverside to a neurosurgeon for an examination. They found that I had a blood spot in the back of my head the size of a baseball. I was taken off work and was given test continually for the next couple of months. Even though I was officially off work I continued to go to the job and do light duty. I went to a seminar in Palm Springs with an assistant that I had known for several years. I could not remember his name to introduce him to other seminar attendees. My memory was definitely deterred.

Approximately six months later our Riverside CSA manager retired and was replaced with another man as manager. This man was definitely a politically motivated individual and his only concern was that the CSA was operated in a politically acceptable method. Whatever the political big wigs wanted they should get it. His main objective was to get all facilities in the CSA signed off, regardless of the conditions, for the developer and accepted by the taxpayers. Due to my physical conditions from the accident, he determined that the CSA should hire an assistant for me. He hired a local farmer as water plant operator for me to teach the operation. Shortly thereafter I had another doctors' appointment in Riverside that took a couple of days. When I returned back to work I found the locks had been changed on the pump stations and on the water plant. I questioned my assistant on this and he said he had been instructed to do that by the CSA Manager. I also discovered that the manager had asked the postmaster at the local post office to give him all of my mail for him to check, which she did. I made a complaint to the United States Post Office inspectors and she was given a severe reprimand. I found that in my absence the manager had the facilities signed off by the authorities, regardless of condition, and ownership assumed by the CSA.

I had a run in with the manager a couple of times. During my five years of employment, schools in the area had been closed by a teachers strike. I had taken a vocal stand on this issue because my children were in school and I did not feel that the students from this district should suffer because some teachers were dissatisfied with their pay or benefits. Their primary object was to have the superintendant fired and the teachers dictate the schools progress and agenda. There was a school board election and I decided to run. The CSA manager told me that I could not run for any political office since I was hired by the county. I politely told him to go to hell. That I would run for any office I wanted to. That was my right as a U.S. citizen. I won the election with a landslide and was elected president of the school board. A local farmer friend of mine also ran and he won also.

There was soon thereafter a shortage of funds in the CSA petty cash. Someone had stolen approximately sixty dollars. The manager called for all office personnel to take a lie detector test. Everyone passed. I found out that he did not take the test, and I notified the Riverside County Manager that all CSA employees felt that it was necessary the CSA manager also take the polygraph test, since he had access to the funds also. I believed he had taken the funds to build a porch on his mobile home. The county required him to take the test and he failed. Everything was hushed up, but I was locked out of some facilities, that I was required access to do my job. I recommended to the County Manager that my job be eliminated and the job title requirements stricken from the records of the CSA. This would prevent anyone else from being promoted to my position. This was done and I left the employ of CSA 51 in late 1973.

I immediately applied for unemployment and was told by the unemployment department that I was qualified as an electronics engineer. In other words, there was no job availability through the employment agency, in our area. I applied for different jobs within the county and in several cities. I was told I was over qualified by each.

I then applied back at MWD for any job available. I got hired quickly at Iron Mountain Pump Station as utility man. There was a big joke among the employees of a utility man coming to work driving a near new Cadillac. My first day on the job the operator called in sick and the plant manager asked me to do high line (230,000 Volt) switching since I was experienced and they were short handed that morning. I did as I was asked without any problems. I still had these orders written down in my notebook from my employment at Hayfield Plant. Thirty days later I was transferred back to Hayfield as the station operator.

I lived at my home in Desert Center (Lake Tamarisk Golf Course) during this time and it was very convenient for my work and to take care of the store also. Lourdes and a couple of clerks ran the store and since I worked the day shift, I could close the store at night. Oweni had graduated from High School and was valedictorian of her graduating class, and I had the honor of giving her diploma as president of the school board. She was going to UC Irvine to college. Thomas would graduate in 1974 and planned to go to college also. Thomas and Ben would help at the store when they were not in school and help to close at night.

During the election to the school board I found how rotten politics could get. Mr. Brown and I were invited, to a teachers' home, one night to discuss our activities on the board. We were unbendable in our opinions of what was needed by the teachers and students. I was sitting on a couch and one lady just happened to fall in my lap and a camera snapped. I knew this was an attempt to blackmail me and I told Lourdes as soon as I got home. Sure enough they tried to show the picture to my wife. She told them where to go, quickly. Mr. Brown and I were then told that something could happen to us. Sometimes people got killed accidently. We went to the District Attorney with this report and were told that since we were public figures nothing could be done.

My children had to pay a high price for my decision to run for school Board. Oweni was given hell by some teachers and some members of the board for writing an article for the student paper supporting actions of the school board. Tom was given some low grades in one class in his final year, to keep him from being valedictorian, because he was my son. I am not sorry for what I did to try to keep the school together as a proper functioning educational institution for the community.

When Oweni was sixteen she got her drivers license. Shortly thereafter I bought a very used Volkswagen Bug for her to drive to school on special occasions. I think the children made two or three trips to high school before it broke down. I had paid two hundred dollars for the car and I sold it for two hundred fifty dollars because it needed a new engine. These models were very popular to make dune buggies. Shortly thereafter we bought her a Datsun sedan. She kept this until she was in college when it was wrecked. After repairs it was not acceptable to me for my daughter to be away at college and use. We bought her a new Nissan Sedan for her school use. I had bought an Oldsmobile Sedan and gave it to Thomas after some time. When he was ready to go to college we bought him a Toyota Station Wagon. The last communication I had from him he still had it. He had an accident one time with it and he came home and I helped him straighten a fender. That is the last time I saw the vehicle. In August 1974 Lourdes bought Ben a new Datsun 240-Z. He used this until he graduated mid year and went to work. He later traded it in for another mode of transportation.

OUR MARKET

During the latter part of 1971 we made a deal and had automotive fuel pumps and twenty thousand gallon storage tanks installed in our store. Some of the prices of fuel at that time might be of interest. Regular gasoline prices were at twenty nine and nine tenths cents per gallon. Shortly thereafter there was a gasoline shortage and I had a one hundred fifty gallon fuel tank installed in our El Camino to guarantee fuel when on the road.

LIFE SADDEST TURN OF EVENTS

In early 1970 we bought a new Cadillac for Lourdes use, and bought a new home at Lake Tamarisk Golf Course, and moved there. Lourdes had always dreamed of going back to the Philippines and driving into her old home town in a Cadillac. I had been travelling a lot and would probably be out of town more as CSA 51 demanded, for the finalization of the water treatment plant. She needed good transportation to meet the store demands in purchasing and banking. In 1974 we traded in the old Cadillac and bought a new one. We had Lourdes initial's engraved on the dashboard in gold. This made her extremely happy. In June she went to San Francisco with Oweni for a visit and a short vacation. They stayed, as I remember, about ten days. We had help at the store and I was there at nights for closing. Tom had just graduated from high school and he would go to college this fall to UCI.

When Lourdes and Oweni got back and the store running normal, it was decided I would take my vacation. Tom, Ben and I made a trip to Arizona, New Mexico, Colorado, Nevada and back home. Our first stop was a motel in Arizona. Tom was disgusted with the motel and went to stay in the car all night. We left early the next morning and went north through New Mexico and on into Colorado. We wanted to take a trip on the narrow gage railway, but there was standing room only. We then decided to take a horseback trip, with a group, up into the mountains for breakfast looking over the railroad. The tourist waved at us cowboys as they went by on the train. Breakfast, cooked on a large piece of tin roofing, was excellent. We went on a ride for most of the day and back to the ranch at night. We spent the night in a motel and wanted to go fishing the next day, but we did not find an acceptable spot. We located an old acquaintance that owned a bar in a nearby town, and visited a short time. We then headed back for California by way of Nevada. On the way back we stopped in Las

Vegas one night. Tom decided to stay in the hotel but Ben and I went out to look the town over. I showed Ben how a slot machine worked. You put in a quarter and get nothing in return. We then went to a McDonalds and got lunch and carried some back for Tom. When we left there the next morning we went home. We were gone about a week. Ben was anxious to get back and enjoy his new car for his senior year in High school. He was a very happy young man with his first car.

When I returned to work, one of the evening operators called in sick. The station chief asked. "will you work over to cover that shift", ie. double shift. I called Lourdes and told her that the scheduled football game they were going to that night would have to be without me. This is the first activity I had ever missed when one of my children were playing. Ben was playing in Arizona that night and Lourdes carried three cheerleaders, a player's mother, and the cheerleader's teacher. I got off work at eleven PM and went to close the store. After I closed the store I went home and checked the cash for the day and went to bed.

About twelve thirty AM on September 29, 1974 the doorbell rang and I answered. It was one of the teachers' wives and she told me that there had been a horrible accident, fifty miles up near Rice, California. I should go immediately to the Parker Arizona Hospital. My car was low on gas and I went to a local Texaco station to fuel up and drove as hard as I could towards Parker. Ten miles up the road I came upon a wreck and one of the school teachers, Mr Reesman, told me Lourdes accident was further up the road. Just before I came into Rice I saw a tow truck picking up our car. They informed me that the ambulance had already taken Lourdes and the passengers to Parker, Arizona. I went there as fast as I could go and when I went into the hospital and asked for Lourdes, she answered from an adjoining room, "daddy I am going to die". This was the most terrible thing I have witnessed in our life together for twenty one years.

There were three other wrecks, in the area, at almost the same time. She got into a room about five AM. Since Tom and Oweni were both at college in Orange County, California, I called them, as soon as I found what the injuries were. Lourdes was severally injured and bleeding internally. The other mother was air lifted to Phoenix, Arizona and died shortly after. The driver, the cheer leader teacher, was critically injured and transferred to Loma Linda Hospital near San Bernardino, California. The cheerleaders were bruised and scared, but with minor injuries. Tom and Oweni got to the hospital in the early morning and insisted that Ben and I go get some sleep, which we did, since we had none for the night. Sometime later, on

September 29, Tom came into our room and said we had better get to the hospital. I later found he had gone to the Indian Reservation to find a Catholic Priest to administer last rites to his mother. Shortly thereafter she was gone. Ben had passed the accident in the school bus but he was not allowed to get out. A school administrator brought Ben to Parker to the hospital after they got back to the school.

Lourdes' funeral services were held in the Catholic Church in Eagle Mountain. The church was full and overflowing into the streets. Burial services were in Coachella Valley Cemetery near Indio, California. I was saddened and depressed beyond anything I had ever experienced. Mrs. Gardener, her friend in San Francisco, came for the funeral and stayed for a few days.

Everyone had come to love her and was very saddened by her loss. The people in the community liked to come into her store and chat with her. All the Kaiser employees looked forward to stopping by at shift change and get beer, soda, chips, etc to eat on the way home. She liked to flip the coin with them for their soda or chips. She usually won. She always had something funny to say to the customers. On several occasions older gentlemen would come in off the highway and ask, where was the beer. Even though they would be sixty, seventy, or eighty years old she would ask them if they were old enough to buy beer. This usually got them to laugh and they would never forget it. Next time they would come through the area, they would stop. Lots of tourist came into the store years later and would ask where the oriental lady was. They all loved her.

Even though she had observed a baby being killed by a Japanese soldier when she was very young she understood that all Japanese were not killers. We had a Japanese engineer working with me when I worked for CSA 51. He was a kind and friendly individual and Lourdes and I became good friends with him and visited with his family in Santa Paula, California. Lourdes liked to have parties at our home and we were friends with Native Indians, Indians, English, Chinese, Philippinos, Hawaiians, and Canadians. She loved to have international parties where each country native would bring a dish of their food.

I took a week off at her death and asked for a year leave of absence from MWD. They refused to grant the leave of absence, therefore I quit. I could not leave Ben, without anyone at home, because he was still in high school. We had the store closed for a week. When it re-opened we had hired help, already on payroll, therefore I cut everyone's hours and started working more time myself. I needed all the help I could get because my brains were not on my work. We had pets at home and I would usually go home midday and lay on the couch. The cat and our dog, Poncho, would join me on the couch. They were as lonely as I. I would try to fix meals for Tom, Ben, and myself. The boys seemed to like sandwiches from the store better than my cooking. I finally almost quit cooking. Tom had quit school and came home because he said I needed help with the store and getting things together.

The vehicle that hit our car was a large Ford van. Two passengers were hurt and the driver killed. There was court cases started. The highway patrol report showed our auto was not at fault. They had been hit, head on, in the ditch on their side of the road. The husband of the lady that got killed in our auto tried to sue us for damages. He lost however because the lady was a guest occupant in our vehicle and our vehicle was not at fault. We tried to recoup damages from the vehicle that hit ours, but they had minimum insurance and the judge ruled that I was still able to work and take care of my children and the poor survivors of the van were injured for life and would have to be re-trained to make a life and the school teacher would be retrained at state expense for another job. We could have appealed but I had gone through enough and just wanted the grief to end.

Due to tax law at that time, I was required to pay inheritance taxes on Lourdes fifty percent interest in the property. We had saved some cash over the years and it took all of our savings to pay off the inheritance tax lien. The law was changed the next year.

On July 4, 1975 weekend, while working in the store with Tom, I came down with a very painful hurt in my abdomen. We had extra help come in and I tried to rest as much as possible. On Monday Ben took me to the doctor. On the way to Indio I passed out. When we got to the doctor he looked at me and told Ben to get me to the hospital. I spent a week in the hospital with kidney stones. When I was released I went back to work. Shortly thereafter Tom stated he wanted to go to Europe for a trip. He had saved up his paycheck and had enough funds available.

Shortly thereafter we had a robbery at the store during busy work hours. A customer grabbed a case of beer and walked out without paying for it or the gasoline he had gotten. He was stopped by the Highway Patrol on Indio grade. I had to go there to identify him and he was taken to Blythe jail by the Sheriffs office. He was later tried and convicted and received thirty days in jail. His father was a Los Angeles police officer.

In April 1976 I came to the store one night to close at 1:00 AM. When I drove up behind the store there was a local young man loitering behind the store. I asked him what he was doing there. He replied that it was not any of my business. I always took a weapon with me when we closed at night and had a twenty two caliber Magnum derringer in my jacket pocket. I pointed my pocket in front of me and told him he should get out of there. He slowly drifted off and away from the property. The Sheriff was called and picked him up, and on questioning the man, the Sheriff was told his intent was to accost the young lady working in the store and assault her. He was sent away for a while because it was one offense of many he was guilty of.

Ben took early graduation from high school because he had the required credits. He then went to work at Bermuda Dunes Airport and got an apartment in Bermuda Dunes close to his work. He liked working at the airport and the customers seemed to like him. He gave good service. He also started going to college at College of the Desert in Palm Desert. He later started his own tanning salon, in Palm Springs, with a partner. He operated this for some time and then made a trip to the northeast coast of the U.S. for a few months. Shortly after his return, Ben changed his name to Thomas A. Falcon, presumably because of a conflict with my name being the same as his. He started his own life at this point because he was now a grown man.

NEW BEGINNING

In the fall of 1975 Ben and Thom both suggested that since Lourdes and I had both discussed taking flying lessons, I should proceed with this. I thought about it and found that I could write off the airplane training expenses if I owned a plane and had it on a rental fleet. I would be operating a business and I must get schooling to operate this business. I therefore found a Cherokee 140 in good condition and purchased it and rented it to a couple of flight instructors for training. I would use it for lessons when it was not in use. I felt this would take my mind off my sorrows and probably keep me alive.

I soloed after four hours of instruction. I then made my first cross country flight to Orange County, Apple Valley, and back to Desert Center. Tom and Ben started taking flight lessons also. I took my written exam and my FFA flight exam as soon as possible. My FAA flight exam was given by an examiner, crop duster, in Blythe. The wind that day was gusting between thirty and fifty miles per hour. I flew into his crop duster airport and he asked, "Do you want to take the test in these wind conditions". My answer was yes, if I could not fly in this I did not need to fly. He took me up and we circled around the Blythe area. He cut my engine and told me to find a place to land. There was a nice cleared farm road just over some power lines. I stretched my flight over the lines. He immediately gave me back power and told me to go around and do it again and go under the power lines. He stated, "Never stretch out a flight when you can get lower and land safer". I flew under the power lines, and after several other exercises, we went back to his airstrip and landed. He complimented me on passing and signed me off for my license on March 28, 1976. I continued to take lessons to improve my flying. I also continued training and flying and later acquired my instrument and commercial license. Flying was my salvation and I enjoyed it very much. It seemed that when I was flying I was closer to God and the heavens and more at peace than any other time. I also rented myself and my plane to others for transportation to any other place they wanted to go. Tom and Ben also continued flying but did not get their licenses. Tom said he just wanted to know how to pilot if he ever had to do it to stay alive. Ben flew with many pilots in many different planes but did not get his license at that time. Some years later he got his license and bought his own twin engine airplane.

I had started going to a local beer bar in the area occasionally, after I closed the store at 1:00 AM, and playing shuffleboard with a friend and drinking a beer. On June 6, 1976 I was enjoying myself in the bar when a young lady stated, "you look like you want to dance". So we danced a couple of dances and I found she was working as the bar tender. Of course the bar closed at 2:00 AM and as I was walking out with one of the mine workers, the young lady was asked if she would like to go to breakfast with us at a restaurant some twenty miles up the highway. She replied, "Yes, I am hungry". She sat next to me while we ate breakfast and I got acquainted with her. I found that her name was Phyllis Rasmussen. She had only been in the area for a short time and had worked at the bar a couple of weeks. I was very impressed with her because she seemed to be very truthful and lonely. She lived in the mobile home park at Lake Tamarisk. I took her back to her vehicle and said goodbye. The next night I went to the bar again and she was there. I again asked her to breakfast, but we went to Desert Center restaurant. After we ate I suggested we go somewhere and just talk. It seemed I was interested in her and it seemed she might have an interest in me. I thought it might be a chance for me to put my life back together; otherwise, I was going to leave the country and do something. I had thought about being a medical flight pilot some where or going anywhere just to get away from my memories. We went out in the desert other nights, and parked and talked for hours, just getting acquainted. I was very impressed because she did not try to be something that she was not or to keep any secrets that I could find.

Phyllis was born in South Dakota and moved to California as a child. Her parents worked in the timber industry and raised their family of six children. Her father was a timber faller (lumber jack) after his time in the service, as a Marine in the pacific theater during World War II. They were a hard working honest family. Phyllis was married before and was divorced for a couple of years. Her marriage was fair for about five years but she found that her husband was gay. He was being mentally abusive to her after some time. Her husband had gone to the same high school as she, and she had known the family. She had enough and it was time to quit the marriage. She had moved to Julian with her sister and family for awhile afterwards.

Shortly thereafter she accompanied me to dinner in Palm Desert at a place that I knew to be very nice. She was extremely nervous that night because she felt it was too fancy for her. We again talked for a long time after we got back to Desert Center, We talked about both of our previous marriages and what we wanted out of life. We even discussed marriage but we both told each other that we did not want to get married. Phyllis got some time off and wanted to go see her sister that lived in Julian, California for a week. I told her that I would take her there with her little Pomperanian dog. She agreed that she would let me do this and I met her sister, Josie, and her family. They owned a small business in Santa Ysabel and lived in Julian. Her sister, Josie and husband, had three sons and I liked them. They were just plain, hard working, people as I was.

When she wanted to come back, I told her I would fly over to pick her up. I flew with the intent of flying into Ramona but changed my mind and looked for a place to land closer in the area. I found what looked like a straight road or a small dirt landing strip about five miles from Santa Ysabel and landed. There was no one at home at the site so I hitchhiked to Santa Ysabel to her sister's store. I spent some time there and her sister brought us back to my plane and we flew back home with her little dog, Mandy. I believe it was Mandy's first plane ride because she seemed very hot and nervous. Of course I probably would have been hot and nervous also if I did not know the pilot or had never flown before.

She had asked her sister Josie what she thought about her marrying a forty five year old man. Phyllis was twenty nine at the time. Apparently her sister thought it would be alright. Phyllis told me she did not love me, but would learn to. We both decided that life could not be more difficult than it was and decided to get married and give it our best efforts. Phyllis had no children and she felt that she could be a good substitute mother for my three children. We flew to Las Vegas on June 26 to get married. We left Desert Center Airport at 6:30 AM and arrived at the Chapel of the Bells in Las Vegas before 8:00 AM. The Chapel took us to the license bureau to get a marriage license and brought us back to the Chapel afterwards. We were one of the first licenses issued that day. After we were married, and the Chapel took our pictures, we decided to go have breakfast together at one of the hotels. We then flew back to Desert Center and arrived home before noon. Phyllis did not seem to be afraid of my piloting even though I was a low time pilot. Oweni had come home from school for the weekend and Tom was already there to meet Phyllis.

TOM AND PHYLLIS MORRING

Ben had met Phyllis before and said he did not want anyone taking his mom's place. I had tried to make him understand that life must go on and that no one could take another persons place in the family or life. As Tom said, we all must adapt to whatever life brings. Oweni went back to college and Tom stayed home for a while and worked the store until Phyllis and I got back from our honeymoon. I made plans to fly to the Hawaiian Islands for our honeymoon. Phyllis had never been there, but I had been there twice when I was in the service. We went to Maui first since I had never been there. We rented a car and made a complete tour of the island from the beaches to the mountains. The most beautiful beaches we had ever seen and the sights in the island were fantastic, the ocean so blue. We went to the bars some, restaurants some, night clubs some, and just got to know each other more, while listening to the beautiful island music. We then flew to Honolulu and did more of the same. We enjoyed one restaurant very much. While you were eating dinner, about twelve stories up, the dining room rotated so you could see a 360 degree view of the city. The food and the entertainment were fantastic. Back in our hotel I decided to sit on the balcony in the sun in my shorts. From this venture I came home with blood poisoning in my ankles from the sunlight. While we were in Hawaii, I wanted to locate a very good friend from my Army days in the Far East. Louis Diaz, Portuguese heritage, had been one of my best friends in the service and had stood by me through lots of hard and scary times. One time when I was wounded he had put one hundred dollars in my pocket as I was hauled away. We could not locate him at all. I could find no evidence of his family on either island. It had been twenty four years since I had last seen or heard of him.

After we got home from our honeymoon Tom went back to college and Phyllis started helping me in the store. Our store hours were now from 7:00 AM to 1:00 AM daily, and business was good. We hired three extra store clerks to help out. I would go to the wholesale grocery suppliers, once per week, and pick up the necessary groceries and supplies needed. We had bought a refrigerated two ton truck for hauling and storing these supplies. We had added additional refrigeration equipment for storage areas also. We had purchased an ice dispensing and storage machine and also a commercial ice making machine. We made and packaged our own ice for sale. We had purchased a three door reach in freezer and had the store so completely stocked it was hard for a large crowd to shop

In about September, Phyllis found that she was pregnant. I have never heard anyone so excited when she called her mom and told her. She was so happy, she had always wanted to be a wife and mother, but it had never happened. On March 25, 1977 our son Brandt Richard Morring was born. His grandmother, Blanche, came down to be with Phyllis when she gave birth. She and I were both at the hospital at that time. She stayed with Phyllis about a week after Brandt's birth, before going back home to Sonora, California. He seemed to always be a very happy and smiling young man. He enjoyed the company of his brother Tom when he would come home. Tom would hold him up to the ceiling with one hand and he would laugh like crazy. He seemed to like this attention and everyone thought he was so cute.

One day Tom was pestering Phyllis and she told him, "leave me alone". He picked her up and put her in the walk in closet. He told her "you said you wanted to be left alone". There were always some practical jokes made and lots of fun and memories for all.

In early 1977 I was notified that my brother, Clyde, had passed away. I immediately flew back to Alabama for his funeral. I was so saddened because I loved him so much and he and his family had always been so good to me all of my life. A strange occurrence happened at the cemetery. My cousin, Carl Morring, Jr. came up to Vivian and me, while we were talking at the cemetery. He told Vivian it was too bad I didn't get to come to the funeral. I was standing next to him and Vivian but he did not recognize me. I had not seen him for twenty years.

Some time later I sold the Cherokee 140 airplane and bought a Cherokee 6 with a 300 H.P. engine. It was much faster and would haul six or seven passengers with full fuel and luggage. It also had more range and could get out of a much shorter airstrip if needed. I also got my real estate salesman license and the airplane was very good hauling customers to Arizona, New Mexico, Oregon, Utah or any place else, to look for land, and fly back to California and write up offers. I also used it to fly miscellaneous family members wherever they wanted to go.

I had a landing strip graded next to the rear of our store property for One Hundred Fifty Dollars. It was approximately sixty feet wide by eighteen hundred feet long and worked fine. I put an aircraft radio in the store in case I needed assistance. At night I could call the store on the radio and have someone put down lights for landing. One time I caught a wind shear, on landing, that blew me into an adjoining ironwood tree and tore my left wing fuel tank off. Another time I lost an engine cowling, just East of Indio, after picking up the aircraft from the Bermuda Dunes Airport Shop but came on to the store and landed. It was at night and Tom supplied lights to land. I later taped up the windshield and flew the plane back to Bermuda Dunes for repairs. Within days of this the same accident happened to an identical model plane on the East coast and killed the pilot.

TOM AND CHEROKEE 6

It was very convenient for flying my immediate family to see their grandparents, bothers, sisters, uncles and aunts and to bring Tom and Oweni home from college in Orange County and Santa Susana (near Van Nuys), California. I also rented it out to qualified licensed pilots that I knew for hauling passengers wherever they wanted to go. I eventually started hauling people most anywhere they wanted to go and anytime they wanted. There was no aviation fuel in Desert Center so I made a portable fuel tank that I could haul and store airplane fuel at my site. I had a 280 gallon portable tank, filter, and pump on wheels for my use. A couple of times we had aircraft going through the area and short of fuel. They would call in and ask if they could purchase some fuel. Of course we served them.

Usually when Phyllis flew with me she would go to sleep soon after we left the ground. She would wake up when she heard me on the radio or when the tires screeched on landing. One time in the Cherokee 140, while over the Palmdale area, I was having trouble trimming the airplane for smooth, level flight. Phyllis was sitting in the rear seat with Brandt. I then realized she was rocking him to sleep. This was causing the small airplane to rock front to back.

In 1978 we got a letter from the family that Tom, Ben and I had visited in Colorado. They had been, previously, Eagle Mountain residents and had been customers in our store and had seen it grow continuously. They had heard that I might want to sell the store. We made an agreement to lease it to them to begin with, and later sold it to them. During the lease period I bought a fifth wheel mobile home and established a real estate office on the north side of the property by the highway. I had to move my airplane to the Desert Center Airport. They did not have the desire to work like we had, and they shortened the hours, deleted the stock, and the store slowly went down. After a couple of years they sold the business to their daughter and son-in-law and it had already gone down too much. They defaulted after approximately one year and we had to take the property back. During this time we had already sold the house in Lake Tamarisk and had bought a new home in Indio, California. After our move to Indio I rented an office there and moved my business address to that area, but I still worked on the sale of land all over the southwest. My airplane had a new home at Bermuda Dunes Airport and I was flying lots more on business.

In our new home in Indio we had made a home for Phyllis dog, Mandy, who seemed to like me very much. When I would come home from work she would meet me at the door. If I did not speak to her and pet her, she would bark at me and stay under my feet until I recognized her. We also got us a cockatiel and his happiest moment was sitting on my shoulder while I took a shower. He was lots of fun and talked a lot. He was missed so much on his demise as was Mandy. They were both such sweet animals. We also acquired a kitten when he was just born. Phyllis had his brothers and sisters in the house and he climbed up my leg and went to sleep in my lap. When the other kitties tried that he slapped them back down. We named him Snuffy and he lived with us for twelve years until he passed. He and Phyllis would play hide and seek around the house and have so much fun.

Thomas had gone back to Orange County to go back to school. He came home occasionally to visit and see how we were doing. Soon thereafter he moved to another residence, but did not give us an address or telephone number. I found that he had a post office box in the county and mailed him some letters. We never got any answers. A private investigator was asked to locate him for us but he later responded with a Los Angles address, but would not provide any other information. He asked that we not inquire anymore through him.

I sent Thomas birthday cards and Christmas cards through 2007, but never got any response even though I requested it. I had sent him checks sometimes for Christmas but the only ones that got cashed were certified checks. Thom and I stopped by his Los Angeles address one time but he was not there.

I cannot remember anything I have done to make him want to break off from the family. He loved his mother tremendously and after her death it seems everything went downhill. I wish him the best in life and hope someday he will surface again before my demise. I love him very much and worry a lot about him.

Relationship with Thomas

BUYING AND DEVELOPING
REAL ESTATE

My lifelong dream had been to own land as far as I could see in all directions and have a home on a hill in the middle of it. I never accomplished this dream but I have tried. I have owned land in Oregon, Wyoming, and California. I, at one time, owned a total of one thousand eight hundred twenty four acres in Desert Center, Blythe, and east of El Centro, Moreno Valley, Desert Hot Springs, Oceanside, California and Wyoming and Oregon.

In the last years at my store property in Desert Center, I had started experimenting with the growing of a new oil bean crop (Jojoba) under a drip irrigation system. I was satisfied that it should work feasibly and hopefully make some money in the future. I had attended many meetings and seminars given by Dr. Yermanos at University of California, Riverside and got to know him personally very well. I had gotten my real estate salesman's license in April 1978. I had the opportunity to buy one hundred seventy nine acres of raw land that had been part of the Desert Center Airport. I later sold the land to a New York investor and he asked me to be a partner in the land. We cleared the land, drilled an irrigation well, and planted it into Jojoba from seed, under a newly designed drip irrigation system. Shortly thereafter I bought twenty acres of land next to my old store property in Desert Center and acquired a partner from the San Francisco area. We had a well drilled there, cleared the land, and planted it into Jojoba under a drip system also. Soon my New York partner wanted to go partners in another piece of land I had for sale in Blythe, California. It already had a well and house on it, but we had to clear the land and install a new drip irrigation system, and plant that also. Before planting that parcel we made a contract to have twenty tons per acre of sewer sludge spread on the land for additional humus and fertilizer.

76

I was seldom in my office anymore but I had one, very good, lady real estate agent that kept the office going in my absence. She was mostly involved in home sales and was a very honest and efficient salesperson. She had a great reputation in the business and was single at that time, so she put in many long hours in our business. My accountant from Riverside shared the office part time so we had coverage while I was out promoting, flying, and seeing the field work got done. During prior years, I was working for a broker from Century 21 and Realty World. While working for him I was awarded salesman of the month for sixteen months out of twenty four. I also was awarded the district second highest salesman of the year, one year, for Realty World in Las Vegas.

Shortly thereafter I went to a seminar in San Diego and distributed my business cards all over the hotel. I met an attorney there and eventually sold him three hundred twenty acres that had been started in grapes by a bunch of hippies and abandoned. It had a good water well and he planted it in Jojoba and asparagus, built a packing shed, fish ponds, and started a new multi farming business. We became good friends and he also worked as my attorney for a while as well as my Real Estate Broker. During the past months I had purchased a trenching machine and he hired me to do the irrigation ditching for the whole acreage. He also bought forty acres, through me, further north and had a well drilled, land cleared, and I did the ditching there also. It was planted into Jojoba and asparagus also. I also acquired lots of Jojoba seed for planting and selling for oil. I sold some of the seed for thirty dollars per pound to go overseas to foreign buyers for planting and oil purposes. The Jojoba oil had a high demand at that time for cosmetic uses and it was also declared a great lubricant for the military.

JOJOBA BEAN PICKER

I then, with some partners, bought three hundred twenty acres in Imperial County, California near Yuma, Arizona. The property already had a water well. We installed a drip irrigation system and planted it in Jojoba. We farmed this until we got our first crop of Jojoba and sold the property. When we got our first harvest I bought a mechanical picker, a modified blueberry picker, and I ran it day and night until harvest was finished. It was too far from home for me to keep it going. I would leave home in Indio about 3:00 AM, go check Desert Center farms, on to Blythe and check farms, on to Yuma area and check farms and get back home sometimes at 10:00 PM at night after having traveled over three hundred miles per day.

I also sold eighty acres North of Desert Center to a couple of business men in Los Angeles. They then hired me to have a water well drilled, plant and farm approximately forty acres in Jojoba for them. One of the partners later died and the property was sold to some oriental partners.

After that I sold a gentlemen from Orange County, California a three hundred twenty acre parcel between Desert Center and Blythe, we made a contract for me to custom plant, and farm it in Jojoba. The parcel already had a water well and had been partially cleared. We trenched it for drip irrigation and planted and grew it for four years until I ran out of steam and gave it up. During this time I had obtained a partner in the farming to take some of my duties off me. I was getting very tired.

At this point I started spending more time selling land as a real estate broker. I had also gotten my Real Estate Brokers License and formed a new real estate company, Desert Gold Realty, and was flying a lot. I had a client that had land in New Mexico that he had been trying to sell for a couple of years through New Mexico brokers. He asked me it I could sell it for him. I flew to New Mexico to see the land, took the listing in California, and found him an eastern buyer. I flew the buyer to see the property, came back to Blythe, California, wrote up the offer and got it accepted and got the buyer back on an eastern plane flight. Everyone was happy. I did this same thing with property in southern Arizona a couple of times as well. One time I had taken two potential buyers to Southern Arizona to view some land. We had to land on a farm field road about six hundred feet long. We looked at the property and they were ready to fly back to Indio. Because of the short strip they said they better hitch a ride back on the freeway. I told them to get in the airplane and shut up. Their problem was that they did not think we could get off the ground with them aboard and that there was a five foot fence at the end of the road and irrigation ditch. I taxied to the end of the road and put on full power and no flaps. Just as we got near the fence I pulled on all flaps and we were well over the fence and on our way. They were both in a sweat. One of the same party, went with me just north of Las Vegas, Nevada to look at some land. We had circled around the whole area at about three hundred feet off the ground when the buyer wanted to know if we were going to land and get something to eat at the nearby restaurant. I replied sure and put on the flaps and prepared to land. He said, "Oh shit". He didn't realize that we were over the runway of an abandoned airport and thought I was going to land in the fields.

Another time I was at a seminar in Riverside and Dr. Yeramnos introduced me to a German buyer. I wrote up an offer on three hundred twenty acres I had for sale and it had to be signed by an attorney in Los Angeles. I had to meet with them for two days to get the deal signed. They offered to pay me six percent commission on the purchase and I had a ten percent listing on the property. The attorney's said I was making too much money and tried for the two days to barter me down. They did not succeed. And it was a good deal for me. The buyers then gave me a contract to get electric power to the property, get it leveled, and a legal easement for ingress and egress, where they desired it to be. For this fee, I got a third trust deed on the property for several thousand dollars. I later traded the note and trust deed for a motor home.

I began occasionally making lectures on growing Jojoba publically to promote the business and answer questions. I gave presentations to the realty board, Autobon Society, and some small groups regarding the growing and potential for Jojoba. I have been mentioned in a couple of articles and Dr. Yermanos had recommended me to several potential growers. Dr. Yermanos published a book on Jojoba and gave me a personal, signed copy. I recommended him to the German growers as an advisor. He later, while in Greece, had appendicitis and died soon after he got back home.

I was also acknowledged as contributor to study of: "Jojoba: New Crop for Arid Lands, New Material for Industry, 1985".

I found that there was not a computerized accounting system for farming yet developed, so I proceeded to write one of my own that was accepted by all of my partners, associates, and accountants with whom I worked.

After growing Jojoba for a while we found that some insects such as grasshoppers, mites, etc. loved to invade Jojoba fields. In looking for a cure we went to University of Arizona and they referred us to an insect grower for the cure. We therefore used aerial sprays, and planted some ladybugs in the fields for the prevention of loss of our plants to insects.

During this period Phyllis had come to work for me in the office since I was absent so much. She was a much needed assistant and did a great job of keeping records and keeping things in order. She had been working at Betty Ford Center, Eisenhower Hospital in Rancho Mirage, California and at J.C. Penny, Palm Desert, California. She was a great addition to our office and very badly needed.

After so many land deals, Phyllis asked, "Please stop buying land". We were always so short of money because of my land purchases. The next opportunity for a land purchase, it was bought in her name, and then I told her. Some short time later she sold it for an enormous profit. Soon thereafter she bought the eighty acres that had been known as Hell, California. There again a good profit was made. She later bought one hundred ten acres near Chiriaco Summit and sold it on terms of ten percent interest for twenty years. I had her hooked by then.

I recently had become more active in the Realty Board. I was soon elected as president of the Coachella Valley East Board of Realtors and also started doing commercial property management of a large medical building. It seems I had to have my plate full of work all of the time to keep me happy. I also received an award as Realtor of the Year. Here again, Phyllis was an enormous help to me and kept me from drowning in paper work.

Later the local Realty Board merged with the Palm Springs Association of Realtors and I served as Director. I was later elected Treasurer of that board and was asked to run for President next term, but I declined because of work constraints and health conditions.

I had been doing land and commercial appraisals for the past several years. I had become accredited as real estate appraiser. I had done several appraisals for Stanley Spiegelman, a superior court receiver, including a date ranch and shop in Indio. I did several land appraisals of different properties in Southern California. On one occasion I did an appraisal for an owner of three hundred twenty acres near Blythe, California that the State of California had decided it needed for a prison. The state appraiser had given a value of three hundred dollars per acre. The property had a new, deep water well with pump that had cost over one hundred fifty thousand dollars. I was asked by the owner's law firm from Riverside to give an appraisal and that I might have to testify in court. My comparable sales and improvements were at three thousand dollars per acre. After several days of court testimony, the owners were awarded three thousand dollars per acre.

I did over thirty large land appraisals on farms and real estate holdings in Riverside County for many clients and reasons.

I did appraisals on estate property in Oregon for California owners. This involved me going to Oregon for several days with my motor home and reviewing the data on that and other properties in the area to establish a value of the estate's property and allowing a sale to be completed.

On another occasion I was requested to do an appraisal of six commercial properties in Las Vegas, Nevada by an accountant. I spent three days doing this work on site and two weeks completing the appraisals. The party I did the appraisals for had a heart attack just as I finished the work and I never got paid the twenty plus thousand dollar fee.

I had done enough land appraisals that I was considered, by the courts, to be an expert witness on land values. Becoming an expert does not require a great academic education or college degree. You need to know how to do research and document the necessary facts. I appeared in Superior Court several times all over Riverside County in this capacity, at the request of various legal firms. I enjoyed the land appraisal business and the opportunities to advance my knowledge both in land values and computer technology.

I also appraised a multi million dollar home in Rancho Mirage, California next to Bob Hope's home for a Los Angeles law firm. This was a gated community on the ridges of the mountains in a very exclusive area. This was the most valuable home that I ever appraised.

APPOINTMENT AS SUPERIOR COURT AND BANKRUPTCY COURT RECEIVER

In 1985 I had joined into a partnership with James Blankenship in two real estate offices under the name of Landvest, USA in Palm Desert and Palm Springs, California. I also brought a young real estate agent, Michael Griffin, into our two new offices. He was the son of a Kaiser Steel Corporation executive that both Blankenship and I knew. Mr. Blankenship had several friends in the real estate profession and he had been involved with several developments, both in the desert and in Las Vegas, Nevada in prior years. Jim was seventy years old and we had some meetings with his associates over the next several months. His associates were an attorney, a banker, a title company representative, an old friend from the Sands Hotel in Las Vegas, and an art dealer. At one meeting he asked me what I thought. I informed him I had no thoughts about his proposed ventures at that time. I was listening and generating my opinions as the different parties discussed them. Some days later he said he did not need me if I did not have an opinion. I told him that was fine, that I did not need him or the group either, I had my own business and reputation already made. Several days later when I came into my office he was sitting in front of my desk and wanted to talk. He said he was sorry about his quick opinion and he wanted to do business, with me involved. Jim got sick and died in December 1986 at seventy two years old.

When Blankenship's will was read he had left a banker and I as administrators of his estate. The banker and I were acquaintances and friends. Everyone that had any recent involvement with Jim seemed to want to sue the estate. One party sued for one hundred thousand dollars for squeezing carrot juice for Blankenship. Two ex-wives sued for all they could get from the estate, just because they could. There was a United States Internal Revenue Service tax lien filed against an associate, and they went after the estate of Blankenship in case he owed funds to one of his associates. I had to lead the battle in the many courts defending his estate. The estate was finally settled after about ten years. His estate involved three hundred twenty acres, and fifty percent of five acres in Carlsbad in San Diego County and, ten acres in Desert Hot Springs, fifty percent interest in five hundred sixty acres in Desert Center, a large condo home in Indian Wells, California, fifty percent interest in three hundred twenty acres in Wyoming, and eighty acres in Oregon. The condo and the Oregon property was sold, the three hundred twenty acres in San Diego was given to the Catholic Church, the Wyoming property was given to a lien holder, and the balance was distributed to the parties that his will instructed, in the percentages that was designated.

In the distribution and sale of these properties I had to go to Oregon to view and appraise the property, go to San Diego County to view and negotiate the distribution of those properties, meet and discharge the attorney that had deemed the estate should have to pay approximately one half million dollars in IRS taxes and hire another one. We estate finally was determined to have one hundred twelve thousand dollars in tax credits.

I was then recommended to the Superior Court of Riverside County as a Court Receiver. I was appointed receiver for a rental residential facility in Indio. When the local police found out I was the Court Appointed Receiver of the property they stated I should have a gun carry permit because the property had such a bad reputation. It was only two blocks from city hall. I did not get a permit nor did I have any problems with the property. The receivership lasted about six months. Next I was appointed receiver on another rental property, used mostly by welfare agencies for their clients. This was an enormous mess. The tenants would move out in the middle of the night and leave truckloads of crap in the buildings. Of course when they were rented they had to be clean, painted and in good condition. Thank goodness this lasted only about nine months. I was then appointed as receiver for a golf cart re-manufacturing business. The Judge called me up at 4:00 PM one afternoon and asked that I take over the business at 8:00 AM next morning. This job lasted about nine months. It was owned by a husband and wife team, and they were fighting. They were both eventually ordered to stay out of the property. They were in court almost every week about something. Of course I had to appear each time. One morning the wife and her attorney came to the business at 8:00 AM to argue with me about something. We argued continuously until noon and they finally left without winning the argument. This attorney later invited Phyllis and I to her home for a Christmas Party and we all had a nice time with many other attorneys and friends.

On another occasion I was appointed to dispose of a property in Blythe, California. I eventually had an auction on the property held in the Blythe Courthouse. Auction started at 8:00 AM, so I took my motor home portable office to Blythe the night before the auction. The auction went as planned. The property was disposed of to everyone's satisfaction.

I had been appointed receiver on a mobile home park near the Salton Sea. The park had sold and the new buyer tried to take it into bankruptcy. I was then appointed bankruptcy court receiver on this case. After the end of the bankruptcy case was settled, I then bought the park, with a partner, from the owner. This proved to be a disaster, because I did not know my partner sufficiently. After many months of work and aggravation, and a heart attack, I sold my interest in the park.

HEALTH ISSUES

In approximately 1993 my family doctor sent me to Loma Linda Veterans Hospital for an examination, since I was a veteran, because he felt that I had some major problems. I went to the VA Hospital for two days and they finally told me that I had a problem, but I would have to go to Long Beach VA Hospital because they could not handle the problem, however, they would not tell me what the problem was. Neither did they tell my doctor what the problem was. He then sent me to another doctor at Eisenhower Medical Center for evaluation and treatment. I had been prescribed Motrin by another doctor twenty years earlier for severe arthritic pain. The current doctor put me on a stronger pain medication and told me to go back to my regular doctor.

In July 1999 we had to clean up a property, of a deceased person, at the Salton Sea. The heirs were my clients. Phyllis, Brandt, and I decided to take care of the job ourselves. It was very hot that day and very humid, 120 Degrees F. and 90+% humidity. In the afternoon I started to feel faint and hurting all over. I told them I was going to go inside the house and lie on the floor for a while. After lying there about one hour I felt some better and we finished the job and went home. For the rest of the summer I had no energy and was short of breath. I had trouble even mowing our yard on the weekends. I would have to stop and rest for a while. I did not know it then, but I had apparently had a slight heart attack at the Salton Sea.

On Saturday December 13, 1999 I had great pain in my arms and chest. I did nothing for the weekend. On Sunday I started convulsions around midnight and decided I was going to the doctor Monday

Thomas? (handwritten)

morning. Phyllis drove me to the doctor's office. When the doctor looked out the window and saw me he told Phyllis to get me to emergency room immediately. We were one block from the hospital. When I entered they looked at me and took me in the examination room immediately. When Phyllis got the car parked and back in the hospital I was already being examined. I was having a heart attack at that time. I was admitted to John F. Kennedy Hospital and put in a bed in the corner of the hallway. All hospitals in the Coachella Valley were full. I was put in an ice pack and left for the night.

Phyllis notified Thom and he came to Indio immediately from Orange County. Oweni came from Iowa and Brandt was already there. No one knew where Thomas was. We had not heard from him in several years. Thom tried for two days to get me transferred to another hospital. Finally they found a bed in Palm Springs and I was transported there by ambulance. There they found that one of my carotid arteries in my neck was blocked and the other one partially blocked. They also discovered that I had partial kidney failure and that could be fatal. They did surgery December 20 and cleared the artery and on December 22 they did a quadruple bypass on my heart. The doctors told Phyllis I had a two percent chance for survival. The operation was successful and I left the hospital on December 27. We then had a nurse visit daily at home for the next two weeks. I was so weak that it was hard to walk across the house. In a couple of weeks I started exercising by walking around the block near our home. A couple of weeks later I started therapy training at Eisenhower Medical Center in Rancho Mirage. This continued until October 2000 and I was feeling very good. A group in Coachella Valley was having a Marathon of 3.7 miles up to the Palm Springs Tramway, a twenty seven percent grade. There were several hundred runners and the winner made it in about twenty seven minutes. He was an African Policeman. Phyllis and I entered the Marathon. We both made it to the top, but we were in last place of the people that continued to the end. There were several heart patients in the therapy class but I was the only one that would attempt the race. Many of the participants in the marathon dropped out without finishing. I was given an award by Eisenhower Medical Center for finishing the marathon.

TOM 10 K TRAMWAY RUN 2000

I had gone back to work, part time, some months earlier. It was apparent that I could not keep the pace that I had been going anymore. I was on heart and kidney medication and had to keep very frequent doctor appointments. I started closing down parts of my business. No more land appraisals, long trips in the desert areas on land sales, no more long daily hours at anything. I was still managing a medical center building and the owners decided to put it up for sale. I sold it in a short time and stopped commercial management also at that time.

My son, Thom and his partner, was building a commercial center of fifty thousand square feet and it was almost finished. They offered me the job of on site management of their facility in Irvine, California. We therefore put out home and real estate business up for sale. The business was sold to one of my agents that had a broker to work with. We had to carry a note back on the business. We also sold our home in Indio and decided to live in our motor home for a while. We put everything in storage that we did not give away. We put our Ford Explorer for sale on a used car lot. We kept Phyllis's

Cadillac for commuting. Brandt had a son and was getting married and had rented a home for his use.

I believed this new management could be done in a forty hour work week and I still had my broker's license and one agent, Michael Griffin, working with me as Landvest, USA brokerage. When Mike went to work with me in 1986 he learned the land business and he has been working, very successfully, in land acquisitions for these past twenty four years. Mike is one of the few people you meet in life that you would not be afraid to give your signed, blank, checkbook. It will be a sad day for me when he is no longer affiliated with my company.

MOTOR HOME TRAVELS

In 1982 we decided to take a vacation and go to a family reunion for Phyllis family in Wyoming. We decided to rent a twenty eight foot motor home and take her mother and father and nephew, Aaron, with us. I believe we were gone two weeks. We met the family at a park in Green River, Wyoming near Flaming Gorge. I do not remember how many family members came but they were from South Dakota, Texas, Oklahoma, and California. We had a great time and made the trip to Jackson Hole, Wyoming one day.

One well remembered time, at the park, there were about twenty of us in a cab over camper just talking and visiting. Someone started telling jokes and experiences over the years. I have never seen so many people enjoy the time so close together. We were telling all type of jokes and comedies from our lives and the camper was just rocking. After the reunion was over we decided to proceed to South Dakota to see some more of Phyllis family and see where she was borne. We also went to Mount Rushmore since we were in the vicinity. We decided on the trip home to start looking for a motor home of our own, since we had enjoyed the trip so much.

We purchased our first motor home, a thirty two foot Executive, in 1983. We purchased it from a gentleman from Wisconsin that had a heart attack in California and could not drive it back home. It was a good 1978 Executive model with approximately forty thousand miles. We enjoyed it very much and put another fifty thousand miles on it until we traded in 1991. We traded for a 1991 thirty four foot Safari with nine thousand miles. This was a good vehicle and we put about fifty thousand miles on it before getting rid of it after fifteen years.

On a trip to Seattle, Washington with the Executive motor home we proceeded towards home via Hwy. 101 along the coast for a scenic view. As we neared the intersection with Hwy. 12 near Aberdeen, Washington we discovered that we had no brakes. We managed to go through the intersection and found a garage nearby to fix our brakes. We were told they might not be able to find parts since the vehicle was getting old. They did find parts in Atlanta, Georgia and had them shipped overnight and we were able to leave the next day. We then proceeded on into Oregon where we spent the night at another RV Park. The next morning I was helping another neighbor hook up his auto to his RV and asked where he got his unit. It was a Safari and he told us that there were some good deals in Eugene, Oregon area where they were made. We thanked him and proceeded south to Eugene, Oregon. We found a good slightly used Safari there and traded for it. On our way home to Indio, California the RV air conditioner quit, but we proceeded on home and communicated with the dealer later. We went to our office in Indio first thing on going home. We went into our office for about an hour. When we came out we found a ticket from the police for having an out of state licensed vehicle. They had seen us come in and knew the RV with the Oregon license belonged to us. I appeared in court, at a later date, for the ticket and explained to the judge that the vehicle was back in Oregon for repairs and the judge voided the ticket.

We were going to take a vacation with the first motor home one year and the engine needed to be rebuilt. The shop did not get it finished in time for us to leave, therefore we made the trip by auto. We visited Sunset Crater National Park in Arizona, then traveled I-40 to Memphis, Tennessee then through Mississippi on to Alabama to visit relatives. We stopped in Corinth, Mississippi to have breakfast. Brandt cracked up when the waitress took our order. He had never heard anyone talk with the slow southern slang before. We then went on to Tennessee to visit my Aunt Flournoy in the hospital who I had not seen for many years. We then traveled through St. Louis, Missouri on to Denver, Colorado, Las Vegas, Nevada and on back home. Phyllis and Brandt thought their butts were glued to the seats. A very long hard trip but nice scenery and visits with family.

We made trips to Oregon, Washington, Utah, Montana, Colorado, Canada, Alaska, Yukon 160 miles from Russia, South Dakota, Nebraska,

Iowa, Indiana, Kansas, Kentucky, Tennessee, Georgia, Alabama, Mississippi, Louisiana, Texas, New Mexico, Wyoming, Missouri, Arizona and over most of California. On one of our trips into Washington state a young man came up to me at a service station and asked if I was Tom Morring. He was one of the Pickle family that had gone to school in Eagle Mountain, California. On another occasion we were in the Yukon sitting at a picnic table and the adjoining people were from Sonora, California where Phyllis' family came from. It is a very small world. We enjoyed the motor home for traveling very much and it was much cheaper than staying in hotels and motels. If you saw a place you wanted to stop, you just stopped and camped for the night or day.

We made one trip from Indio through Arizona on I-10 to Columbus, Georgia to visit an old friend and real estate associate, then on to Huntsville, Alabama to visit my nephew, Billy and Eva Morring and niece, Ann and Jerry Sanderson. We then went through Memphis, Tennessee and on to visit my daughter, Oweni and family in Ankeny, Iowa. After staying there for a few days we then went west through Wyoming. We ran into severe wind there, with Phyllis driving, and she turned it over to me. We went a short distance until we found an RV park and stopped for the rest of the day. Winds were forty to fifty miles per hour and very unsafe to drive with a large vehicle. The next day we left there and proceeded to Santa Rosa, California to visit more family and then proceeded home. On the way through San Francisco we encountered a U.S. Postal Service truck parked well into the street and very heavy traffic going both ways. I tried to go through the narrow lane that was left and knocked off the mirror on both the postal truck and our motor home. There was no place to stop, therefore we proceed on home.

Once again we took a cross country trip to see our daughter and family in Ankeny, Iowa. We had a breakdown near Grand Island, Nebraska and had to be towed to a garage and fixed. There was a short delay because the breakdown had happened in early day. We then proceed to Ankeny, Iowa for a few days. Oweni, Steve, and family took us for a grand tour of Iowa. There were many nice areas and people to visit. We had never been in that area before. We then went on to Huntsville, Alabama to visit our nephew and family. We stayed there for a few days and then proceeded on to near Fairfield, Texas to visit Phyllis' Aunt and family for a day or two. We then proceeded home via I-10.

CRATER LAKE OREGON

BUFFALO YELLOWSTONE

CODY WYOMING

On another occasion we took a RV trip, towing our Ford Explorer, to Billings, Montana via Montague, California to visit Phyllis' sister and family, then to Crater Lake, Oregon on to Spokane, Washington then to Coeur de Lane, Idaho to Missoula, Montana to visit some friends, and then to Red Lodge, Montana where we parked for a few days in an RV park. We then decided to view Yellowstone National Park for a few days and then went on to Cody, Wyoming to see a rodeo and other sights in our Ford Explorer, then back to our coach. We proceeded to Billings, Montana for a few days and then left for Denver, Colorado. About fifty miles south of Billings I felt a jerk on the RV and saw the Explorer jerk to the left and then knew we had lost it. The ball on the hitch had broken and the Explorer was off on the right side of the highway. An auto that had been following us stopped and asked if we needed help and I called the Highway Patrol. They sent out a tow truck but the only severe damage was a destroyed tow dolly. Phyllis drove the Explorer behind me until we got to a town and rented a new tow dolly and had it installed. We then proceeded on to Denver to see an old neighbor and friend that we had not seen for a few years.

On another trip to Palo Alto, California for a second cousin's wedding, Phyllis cooked breakfast in the motor home, for between thirty and forty people. We were parked in a motel parking lot and the whole reunion enjoyed breakfast in the motor home. Many said this was a first and complimented Phyllis for having such a great facility for traveling.

We went to Ventura, California area beaches many times where we could park right by the beach for six dollars per night. One morning we were having coffee under out awning and Phyllis set her cup on the ground and went back in the coach for something. A squirrel came up and nosed around and found her coffee. He drank most of the balance in the cup before running away. The next day he was back again and came into the motor home and had his coffee on the floor by the door and looked around and visited the coach before running away. We thereafter fed them every morning until we left. There were always sea gulls and squirrels around begging for food. This was an enjoyment to relax, read, walk the beach, and feed the animals. On one other time a man knocked on our door of our coach about 3:00 AM and woke us up. After telling him to go away several times, and his persistence, I told him if he knocked again, and did not go away, I would shoot him through the door. He left and we were not bothered again. Phyllis' sister Josie was with us one time and we had a nice relaxed visit on the beach for a few days.

We took another vacation to northern California and took Phyllis mother, Blanch and her Aunt Violet from Santa Rosa, California with us up the coast to Bodega Bay. We parked in a park near the beach one night and had been playing the television quite a lot. The next morning the motor home battery was dead. Everyone wondered what we were going to do since we were quite a ways from town. My brains started working and I remembered we had a bypass switch and could start the engine from the coach batteries. We stopped and parked along the coast on Hwy. 1 for a couple of days, just viewing the area and enjoying the peaceful time without anyone around. We then proceeded up the coast to Ft. Bragg, California then over to Hwy. 101 near Willits, California and back to Santa Rosa for Aunt Violet's home. We then proceeded back home. Along with all of these motor home trips were many tire blowouts and flats to have fixed. Due to the fact our coach sat parked for most of the year the tires dry rotted from no use.

In 1992, the fiftieth anniversary of the Alaska Hwy. (Alcan Hwy.) we decided to make a trip to Alaska and the Yukon to see the historic places along the route while our motor home was near new. I had been to Anchorage, Alaska for four hours, while in the military. I especially wanted to go to Dawson, Yukon, the area of the Jack London stories in history. We decided to leave in mid July and to be back to work by mid to late August.

We left Indio, California and proceeded on to Interstate 5 through Washington State to near Linden, Washington where we crossed the Canadian border. We had stopped in route and bought some pears to eat on the trip. At the border crossing we were informed we could not take fresh fruit, of any kind, into Canada. We had the choice of giving them the fruit or pulling over and eating it. I was not about to give away perfectly good fruit, therefore we pulled over and ate the fruit and then proceeded on our way. We followed Canadian Highway 5 through British Columbia to Kamloops. While in Kamloops we heard on television that there had been an earthquake in Yucca Valley, California. We called our neighbor and enquired about damage. She reviewed our house and found that only a clock had fallen. We then took Highway 97 to Prince George, then Highway 16 west to Kitwanga. This was a beautiful country with forest, lakes, small villages, etc. We saw some baby bears and lots of fishing camps along this route. There were lots of float planes on the lakes near fishing camps.

We then took Highway 37 northwest to Meziaden. Along the way we started to have engine problems. We continually lost power in our engine and a highway repair crew advised us to take Highway 37A to Stewart and Hyder, Alaska. We found a garage in Stewart and they found that our catalactic converter was plugged, even though the unit was almost new. The garage found one in southeastern Canada and had it shipped overnight. While we were waiting we walked to Hyder, Alaska and looked around. The next day our unit was repaired and we proceeded back to Meziaden and then proceeded north along Highway 37 to Yukon Highway 1 near Watson Lake. This was again beautiful country, but very remote. We had seen small bears again and some moose and elk. We followed Highway 1 west to Whitehorse, Yukon Territory where se stopped to do some laundry and rest some, from the twenty five hundred mile drive.

GLACIER NEAR HYDER ALASKA

The self service laundry was very expensive. It cost us twenty five dollars to clean and dry our laundry. We had a nice visit to the town and rested in a large RV park for a day. We got acquainted with a family from Sonora, California; Phyllis parents latest home. It is again a small country. We visited around the town and just relaxed for a day.

We then decided to go northwest via Yukon Highway 2 to Dawson City, Yukon Territory and visit the area of so many of Jack London's story books. We did view the home of Jack London and many other well documented facilities around town. We pulled into a Chevron gas station and the young boy, approximately fourteen years old, asked if we wanted to fill up the motor home. When I said yes, he yelled out, "They want to fill it up". We took on about eighty five gallons at almost three dollars per gallon. It was so much that Chevron called to verify the amount on my credit card. This was the most expensive gasoline I had ever purchased for automotive use to that date. The station gave Brandt wall posters and a lot of stuff for the purchase.

JACK LONDON HOME DAWSON YUKON

DAWSON YUKON

DAWSON YUKON

FISH CAMP GARDEN YUKON RIVER

ALASKA YUKON BORDER
TOP OF THE WORLD HWY

TOP OF THE WORLD HWY

MUSK OX ANCHORAGE ALASKA

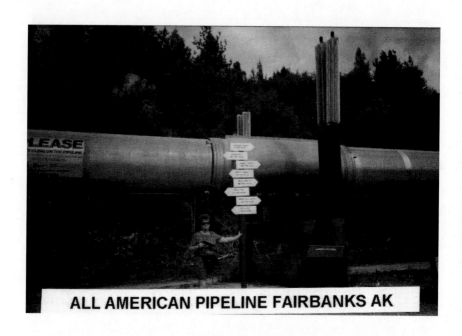

ALL AMERICAN PIPELINE FAIRBANKS AK

GOLD PANNING FAIRBANKS AK

We stayed there several days and went on a trip up the Yukon River to a fish camp for dinner one day. It was a delicious salmon dinner accompanied with fresh vegetables grown in their own garden on site. On the trip up to Dawson City, I had been driving all day and the family asked if we going to stop sometime. It was past 1:00 AM and still daylight so I was still driving. It was very odd to have the nights so short. After viewing most everything in town it was time to move on.

We took Highway 9 across the Yukon River, by ferry, to connect to Alaska Highway 5 (the Top of The World Highway) and south through Chicken, Alaska. We stopped in Chicken and mailed letters and cards home from their ten by ten foot, unmanned Post Office. We then proceeded on to Tetlin Junction, Alaska and connected with Highway 2 (the Tok Cutoff) to Tok, Alaska where we picked up Highway 1 on to Glennallen, Alaska and then to Glenn Highway on to Anchorage, Alaska. Near Palmer, Alaska we stopped and viewed a field of Musk Ox. They were very interesting to watch and we were told a story about them and their history. We viewed Anchorage for a couple of days via tours, and then took Highway 3 to Fairbanks, via Denali National Park and Mount McKinley (the highest point in North America, over 20,000 feet). We took tours around Fairbanks and to see the All American Pipeline and some gold mining. We even tried our hand at gold panning, no luck of course. We also again saw some Caribou crossing the road and were told and shown some historic points around town.

We then proceeded via Highway 2 (Alaska Highway) to Delta Junction, Alaska where we stopped to view a Russian Air force, demonstration fly over. We then continued on southeast through Tok, Alaska to connect to Yukon Territory Highway 1 near Beaver Creek, Yukon. We pulled off near Kulane, Yukon to rest and our motor home locked up in neutral and we could not proceed. I tried to call for help on our CB radio but got no answers. Brandt and I walked down a forest road, which looked like it had daily use, in hopes of finding someone. We had no luck and just as we got back to our motor home some ladies pulled into the area. They got someone on their CB radio and called us a tow truck. We were about forty miles from Kulane and the service truck towed us there for repairs. The belt drive from our air conditioner had broken; therefore we had no power to take our automatic transmission out of park. The service garage bypassed our air conditioner and we were able to go on our way after spending the night.

BREAK DOWN 50 MILE TOW

BREAKDOWN AREA

We then proceeded on our way via Yukon Highway 1 to Whitehorse and then on to Watson Lake, the location of the Signpost Forest. We stopped at the Signpost Forest to view the many thousands of signs, from all over the world, that had been put up by visitors from the many places. We had a sign that Brandt had made in high school woodshop on our dashboard in the motor home of the Morring name. He decided to put our sign on display there also, to let anyone know we had been there. I am sure it is still there today.

MORRING SIGN SIGN POST FOREST

SIGN POST FOREST WATSON LAKE

Watson Lake, Yukon. The world famous Watson Lake Signpost Forest was started in 1942 by a homesick U.S. Army GI, Carl K. Lindley of Danville, Illinois. While working on the Alaska Highway he erected a sign there, stating mileage to his hometown. Others followed his lead and are still doing so this day.

We proceeded on along Yukon Highway 1 to the connection with British Columbia Highway 97 through Dawson Creek on through Prince George to Cache Creek where we turned further south to Highway 1 to Hope and southwest to Abbotsford and across the border to Lynden and on Interstate 5 at Bellingham, Washington. From there we took Interstate 5 back to Los Angeles and then back home to Indio, California and lots of rest. We had driven over six thousand five hundred miles in twenty nine days.

It was a great trip but Phyllis description of the trip was six thousand miles of bad road. I have not hears any comments out of Brandt, but I thought the trip was great and very educational. Phyllis made the comment that the trees were so small. She had thought they would be very large. I think she enjoyed the trip more than she realized. The road conditions were caused by the permafrost (freezing) in long winter months and then thawing in summer. Your rear axle differential dragged the ground in many places along the road. You just had to follow the wheel ruts made by other vehicles.

We were told on one occasion that some California residents had come into Fairbanks, Alaska area and bought some land and proceeded to build a house. They were told by the local residents and engineers that they needed to drive down pilings through the permafrost to stabilize the home or they would have trouble. They proceeded to build without the pilings and the next summer their house settled and was destroyed when the earth thawed. There is always something to learn by listening to the residents of an area.

MOVE FROM DESERT AREA

In March 2001 we moved from the desert to Orange County. We rented a space near the beach in Newport Beach, California at a great, but expensive RV park, for fourteen hundred dollars per month plus utilities. The cooler weather was much enjoyed after fifty plus years in the desert area. My routine, at first, was to go nine miles to the property in Irvine, check it out, correct or advise on any difficulties, go to the company office on Main Street near John Wayne Airport and do the necessary book and computer work.

After a year we bought a mobile home in a senior mobile home park, in Lake Forest, with all amenities. In doing this our space rent and utilities were about a thousand dollars per month. I was then living about two miles from my work. It was much closer if I got an alarm call in the middle of the night. The park had many amenities for its senior citizens; dances, parties, recreation room, pool and etc. We also had to buy a new vehicle, a 2002 Mazda Tribute, to replace Phyllis' Cadillac that had decided it was time to quit. I was using the Tribute for my work therefore Phyllis had to walk where ever she needed to go. She had to walk about two miles to get to the stores, library, malls, etc. and activities she wanted to participate in. This took a lot of her time and energy but she didn't complain. She liked being out of the desert.

Thom gave Phyllis an electric bicycle to assist her in getting around town when I was at work. If you ran out of battery power you could peddle the bike. It ran out of power one time on Phyllis when she was about a mile from home and it was too heavy for her to peddle with her merchandise. That was her last trip away from home with it.

In 2006 we bought a condo at a senior citizens development in Mission Viejo, California. The previous owners had passed away and their son had to get rid of it because he was not a senior citizen. We had sold some land in Moreno Valley, California to the Riverside Conservancy for less than market value and did an IRS 1031 Exchange for the condo. We also were given a plaque with a painting of the land by the Conservancy. The property we bought was in good shape but at the top of the real estate market at that time. We made the purchase in June 2006 and had a patio cover installed, wood floors, and had it painted throughout. The senior development, Palmia, had upscale homes and condos, recreation facilities, pools, libraries, lake access and all types of amenities for the enjoyment of senior citizens. It was a very quiet and security conscious development with security gates and guards on duty twenty four hours per day and was extremely quiet. It is a real joy to live in and be a part of the community even though I am not a social animal. I usually keep to myself and try to tend to my own business.

Due to the fact that out new home was eight miles from my work, I decided to buy me a 2007 Ford Explorer Sport Tract, for my work vehicle since I sometimes needed to haul tools and supplies for work or take care of my real estate duties. This would give Phyllis a vehicle, the Mazda, if she needed something when I was not at home. She could also use this to go to doctors' appointments, shopping, etc. This was needed and pleased Phyllis very much. She loved the Mazda and liked to drive it and felt safe in it.

My property management job was ended April 30, 2009. I had a lot of personal real estate matters to finish for the next few months, even though I was not totally retiring. I also had many medical appointments to keep so the second auto was still needed.

We finally sold the Mazda in May 2010. I had gotten an estimate from the Mazda dealer and CarMax. We sold the car to Mazda since CarMax offered us twenty five percent less. The Mazda was eight years old with sixty three thousand miles, but we just did not need two vehicles anymore.

I am still trying to sell more of my land in Desert Center and we have to go there occasionally. The area seems to deteriorate more each day. I have been trying to interest the Solar Industry in the land. Years age Desert Center Service and Supply, Inc. offered free room and board any day the sun did not shine in Desert Center. I know they did not have to provide this to anyone for over 5 years while I worked there.

One of the most beautiful things about the desert is the sunshine three hundred sixty five days per year, quietness, and the winter climate. The summers get miserable unless you change your schedule to work very early and quit about one in the afternoon. I worked this schedule for about forty three years.

CHANGING WORK LOCATIONS
AND DUTIES

I worked at this property management job for eight years until May 1, 2009 when the property was sold. The new buyers wanted a major commercial brokerage to manage the property. I had done previous property management services, including accounting, with property management software that was known nationwide. When I started in Irvine I was asked what bookkeeping program I used or was familiar with. I went to Texas, to an update Tenant Pro bookkeeping school, to get the latest amendments that had been made to the system. One of the owners also did bookkeeping on other aspects of the business with QuickBooks. The fee for the update school was paid for her to go also, but she declined to go.

The properties had computerized alarm systems with electronic key entry, computerized air conditioning/heat pump control systems on all forty four separate heat pump systems. Part of my duties were to keep tenants supplied with usable entry codes for the alarm and entry systems and to monitor and control all heat pump systems twenty four hours per day. I also did the billing for the tenants, paying venders, making deposits, and doing budgets for the properties, and minor maintenance that I could do.

Everything went fine for about five years regarding the bookkeeping. I was then told that I would have to change bookkeeping systems, to QuickBooks, four months into the year because no one knew the system I had been using. I refused to change, stating that I was too old to learn another system, and the owners gave the bookkeeping to another lady in the office. She immediately tried to undercut my authority as manager in every way possible and told the tenants she was the new manager. I told the owners that I felt that I should quit since I did not have any authority anymore. It seemed that everything I did was wrong or owner's stated I did not know what I was talking about. I was asked to stay on. After about two years the new office lady had burned her bridges and decided to leave in a month. She was immediately discharged. The bookkeeping was then assumed by one of the owners. It was still kept as secret as possible from me as manager, therefore I had to start keeping important parts of the records for my own information. It is impossible to answer questions from tenants, about the upkeep and costs, when you do not have availability of the records and from venders when you do not know if they have been paid or not. It was definitely a relief to leave the facility, even though I enjoyed the job most of the years I had been there.

In early spring the owners would supply the tenants with donuts, bagels, and cream cheese for a treat. In mid year we would have a lunch for the tenants by Wahoo's Fish Tacos or In-Out Hamburgers catered on site. During my tenure we had Christmas parties each year for the tenants. We rented a boat for a tour of the Newport Bay at Christmas time when the bay was all lighted up for the holidays. There was a dinner, bar, dancing to karaoke songs and music, and general visiting by all tenants for three to four hours in the evening. The tenants loved these treats and asked each year, before the time, if we were going to have them.

One time at Christmas a Korean, visitor of one of the companies, asked is I had served in Korea. I stated that I had and he thanked me so greatly for serving to free his country, that it brought tears to my eyes. It was the first time anyone had thanked me for our service there. He was about 45 or 50 years old. It made a great day for me.

In May 2006 the owners gave a party for the tenants and included a seventy fifth birthday party for me. They had a cake made with me in my army uniform as a young man about fifty three years earlier. It was a nice party and enjoyed by all. One of the tenants, Exponent, gave me a gift certificate for one hundred fifty dollars at a nice restaurant in Corona Del Mar, California. We took advantage of this certificate on our thirty third wedding anniversary on June 26, 2009.

In July 2006, Thom gave us a trip to Maui in the Hawaiian Islands for all of our immediate family to celebrate a reunion and Phyllis and my thirtieth anniversary. All of the family was there except Thomas, including our grandkids. We had a great time eating, sleeping as long as you want, traveling, swimming, and whatever. We took one under water trip along the bay in a submarine. The grand children had a great time trying surf boarding and lots of swimming and eating. This was a new adventure for all of us and quite educational and informative.

It was a great vacation and family gathering. We had been to Hawaii for our honeymoon and had visited Maui. There were so many changes there in the thirty years, just like the rest of the world. When you stay in one area for so many years you do not realize the rest of the world has changed so much. Maui had become so commercialized over the years that nothing looked familiar.

MORE HEALTH ISSUES

Due to my knee and leg injuries I was unable to take a normal stress test to analyze my heart condition. The doctors had been giving me a chemical stress test since 2001 to determine heart conditions. In early 2002 my right knee began hurting severally while walking and climbing, and at night. The doctor said the knee joint had deteriated to the point that it would have to be replaced. The joint had apparently been damaged due to the fact that I had lost a kneecap and other injuries, from the left knee in 1955, which had put more use and stress on the right knee.

Due to my heart and kidney problems and a very low blood count the knee replacement was put off for several months. I had been prescribed for a shot of Procrit every three weeks for the past one year due to low blood count. I finally had it replaced on April 1, 2004. I was back working and walking, without a cane, within two weeks. The knee worked well and I continued therapy for about six months. The knee recovered with approximately one hundred ten degree flexibility. The normal flexibility of a knee is approximately one hundred thirty degrees.

After the knee surgery I was hallucinating and thought I was in a hospital in Bagdad. I told Phyllis, when she said she was going home, that I did not believe they would let her leave because of the danger of the trip. I had been listening to the Iraq difficulties prior to the surgery and thought I was there. I spent approximately five days in the hospital and went home.

My heart and kidneys were improving or holding stable until July 2008 when I starting losing blood internally and my blood count got very low. The doctors gave me so many tests, to find the problem, that I lost count of the test. I was admitted to the hospital, and given two pints of blood, and released. I had to take about a month off from work because I was so weak. The doctor eventually had me swallow a camera that took pictures of my stomach, small intestines, and large intestines. The doctor said there was not any problem observed, but there were several red spots that probably indicated there had been bleeding. There have been no problems since, to date. I was taken off aspirin (325 MG) which had been prescribed for me for the past eight years.

On Christmas Eve 2008 I was unloading a case of bottled water from my truck and lost my balance and fell backwards with the case of water in my arms. I was unable to get up with out assistance. I called Phyllis on my cell phone to come and help me. It took approximately three months for my back to recover and get stable again. From that time on I quit lifting anything of significance.

My blood counts and heart condition have held stable since that time. In August 2009 the Procrit shots were discontinued because blood count was holding just below normal and heart and blood pressures remained stable. I was also taken off several other medicines near this time and everything seemed to hold stable. The Procrit was started again in January 2010, since my blood count was low again.

In mid August 2009 I apparently had, and passed, another kidney stone. My doctors' appointments had been extended to every two and four months apart. Health was progressing fine for my age. I also noticed that my short term memory was declining considerably. I am sure this is due to age and medicine since everything wears out. Any day that I get up and see sunshine is a great day.

In December 2009, while visiting Thom, in Healdsburg, California, I tried riding a Segway Human Transporter. I had seen these in use by security personnel at shopping centers and some few on the street. Naturally, I had to try this vehicle. Thom had one with larger tires that was used off and on road. Everything was fine until I lost by balance, which had been declining but I refused to acknowledge. In losing balance the vehicle automatically reversed and I hit the ground. I could not get up without help and Thom advised me to stay down because it looked like I might have a broken leg. Sure enough it was broken in three places and was my right leg with the replaced metal joint therefore it had to be prepared for healing the old fashion way which takes about six months normally.

I was taken to the hospital in Healdsburg and later moved to Santa Rosa Hospital where my leg was set as best possible and put in a cast to my hip. The next day I was moved to a friend of Thom's home, until we could come home to Orange County. We were eventually flown home by air accompanied by Thom and his friend. Thom had our automobile ferried back to us by a friend.

We went to our orthopedic surgeon shortly and had the leg analyzed. He did x-rays and replaced the cast and I went home bedridden for the next two months. Phyllis job then became nursemaid, chauffeur, and baby sitter in addition to being a wife. It was very hard on her but she did not complain. After this period the doctor replaced the cast with a shorter cast for the next two months so that I could bend my knee.

During this period I had other medical problems with my kidneys and was put on other medication as well. This created additional problems and I had to discontinue the medication. I lost about ten pounds and was very weak both physically and mentally. Finally the doctor removed the cast and put me on two months of physical therapy, twice per week. I have now been dismissed after six months and the doctor said I was doing well, but the leg would take approximately two years to heal completely.

I certainly do not want to try this again. It has been a long hard journey at this point in life, but I made it. I am still just as ornery as ever, but I just have to move a lot slower.

During this six months Phyllis found someone in Lake Forest with a mobile electric chair to give away. It was about eight years old but it had been kept in the house and in good condition. They gave it to us and Brandt installed new batteries and serviced it for me. It worked great and I used it for about three months. I still have it on standby because I know the time for my need again is ahead.

We started painting the inside of our condo in June 2010 and I quickly determined I could not climb ladders; therefore the high and low painting was left to Phyllis. About the first week in July she fell of a low ladder and injured her back. The painting was put on hold until her back recuperates. We went back to painting in August and finally finished the job. This will definitely be the last time we do this painting ourselves.

The doctors now find that I am holding stable physically but I cannot walk very far. Doctor visits are now every four to six months for the first time in ten years.

RETIREMENT

The day has finally come to retire and hang it up. I have worked hard and long hours most of my life and I am not sure retirement fits my agenda, but I guess seventy nine years of age must be enough. I still have my real estate broker's license and have one agent working with me. He is doing all the work. I am keeping all the records and giving what advice I can. The agent, Mike Griffin, has been with my company twenty five years and is one of the most trustworthy people I have ever known. We have been through lots of good and bad times together.

The property I had been managing for the past eight years was sold the last of April 2009. My last day was April 30, 2009. The new owner's agents asked if I would consider staying on as site manager. I gave them a price for working twenty hours per week and the owners stated they did not want me. The new owner's agents were given all current records and instructions for the air conditioning, alarm, and security systems. Three weeks later the agents called and asked if I would put changes of security cards in the security system since they did not know how to do it. I had already removed the systems from my computer, therefore I responded that I could not. One of the prior owners called and asked if I would give the new management company my computer in exchange for a new one. I told him it would not be of any use to them as I had removed all programs concerning the buildings. Approximately three weeks later a new security company called and asked me to let them into the facility so they could service and install new systems. Apparently they could not get into the facility and said the management company did not know how to let them in. They were told that it was their problem and I had no access to the facility.

I continued to get calls, communications, e-mails, etc. from tenants, vendors, service companies, and City of Irvine, weekly through October

2009. I provided all tenants, venders, city, power suppliers, etc. letters regarding change of ownership prior to my departure.

 I feel in retirement that I have lost most of human value. You are too old to work; you do not know anything, physically unable to do most anything. What value are you to society?? I feel that you are now a burden to society if you cannot contribute more since you are supposed to be older and wiser. Even our current government leaves the opinion that since you have provided all you can to society, it may be time to let us go back to our maker.

I have done so many things in my life and experienced so much. My life has been very full, and very interesting. I have lived up to many of my dreams and tried to help many people live up to theirs. There have also been many disappointments, that is life.

I have been extremely lucky and had as my partners two of the most loving, faithful, and wonderful women in the world as wives. They came to me from totally different parts of the world and under very different circumstances. The both have born me fabulous children and taught them the responsibilities of life when I was away working at many varied jobs and labors.

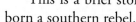 They both served as complete caretakers and nurses for many months when I sustained injuries in accidents. No one could ask for more out of life even though I wonder why I did not do more. There has been so many opportunities that I have passed by and I wonder what they might have been had I taken advantage of them.

I am spending my time now trying to leave a summary of my life for my children and grand children since they may not have known the history of my being or any accomplishments I have made. I hope it is enjoyable for them, and anyone, to read and dream of their past and future.

This is a brief story of my rebellious dash of life in addition to being born a southern rebel.

THE MORRING FAMILY ANCESTRY

The Morring family history, from information told to me, began in Scotland as three brothers came to the United States. One of the brothers stayed in the Kentucky area and the other two came into the area known as Alabama. George Webb Morring, my great grandfather was born 20 May, 1793 in Virginia, deceased 30 July, 1874. He married Diana Gwathney born 1805 in Virginia, deceased 28 February, 1844 in Madison County, Alabama. They had eight children, one of which was Thomas Jefferson Morring.

Thomas Jefferson Morring, my grandfather was born January 10, 1842 in Jackson, Alabama, deceased January 29, 1908. He married Mary Augustus Lawler on December 6, 1871. Year of birth 1854, deceased 1921. They had five children, Benjamin Thomas Morring, Sr., Bruce Morring, Carl Agustus Morring, Mamie Morring Miller, and Jimmie Morring Anderson, all now deceased.

Benjamin Thomas Morring, Sr. married Mattie Lawler and they had two children, Alta Morring and Clyde Benjamin Morring, both now deceased. Alta Morring had one child, Robert Morring. Clyde Morring married Vivian Acuff and they had three children; Alta Ann Morring-Sanderson, Billy Clyde Morring, Bruce Roger Morring. Bruce is now deceased. Benjamin Thomas Morring, Sr. later married Mackie Maye Oene Williams and they had one child, Benjamin Thomas Morring, Jr.

Benjamin Thomas Morring, Jr. married Lourdes Diangson of the Phillipine Islands and they have three children; Oweni Lourdes Morring, Thomas Norberto Morring, Benjamin Thomas Morring, III (aka Thom Falcon). Lourdes Morring was born January 29, 1937 and deceased September 29, 1974. Benjamin Thomas Morring, Jr. later married Phyllis Ann Rasmussen and they had one child, Brandt Richard Morring. Oweni Lourdes Morring married Steven Henry and they have two children; Grady

Diangson Henry and Sally Morring Henry. It is unknown if Thomas Norberto Morring is married or has any children. Benjamin Thomas Morring, III (Thom Falcon) is unmarried. Brandt Richard Morring married Melissa Brannen and they have two children; Skylar Brannen and Seth Ray Morring.

THE WILLIAMS FAMILY ANCESTRY

The early history of the Williams family is unknown to me. My grandfather, Henry Harrison Williams was born November 11, 1857. He passed away on October 13, 1944. He married Mary Elizabeth Burch on October10, 1888. She was born September 8, 1869. She passed away March 11, 1938. They had six daughters, Verna Eloise Williams, Georgie LeVert Williams, Mackie May Oene Williams, Mable May Allene Williams, Douglas Irene Williams, Flournoy Elizabeth Williams. Verna Eloise Williams married John C. Barlor and they had four children; Henry Hilliard C. Barlor, Jerome Barlor, Luree Barlor, Evelyn Barlor. Georgie LeVert Williams, Douglas Irene Williams, Flournoy Elizabeth Williams remained single for life. Mackie May Oene Williams and Mable May Allene Williams were twins born August 30, 1985. Mable May Allene Williams married J. Sam Smith and they had one son, Dr. Fredrick Williams Smith. Mackie Maye Oene Williams married Benjamin Thomas Morring and they had one son, Benjamin Thomas Morring, Jr.

Why push yourself so hard?